HEALTHY

NINJA CREAMI

PROTEIN

COOKBOOK

1500 Days of Easy and Simple Low Calorie, Plant based, High Protein Ice Creams, Milkshake, Sorbet, Smoothie, Gelato for Beginners and Advanced Users

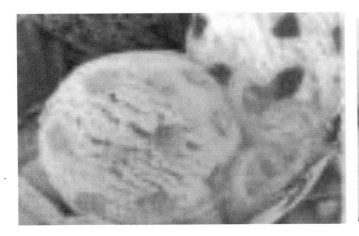

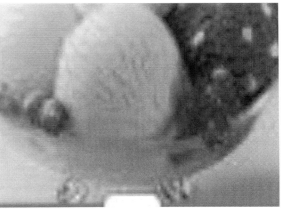

CAROLYN A. BISHOP

ABOUT THE BOOK

Whether you're a fitness enthusiast, a busy parent looking for nutritious snack options, or simply someone who loves indulging in delicious desserts without the guilt, this book is crafted just for you.

Using this cookbook is as much about embarking on a culinary adventure as it is about achieving your health and fitness goals.

- **Familiarize Yourself with Your Ninja Creami**: Before diving into the recipes, take a moment to get to know your Ninja Creami Deluxe. Understanding its features and functionalities will help you achieve the best results. If you're new to the Ninja Creami, a quick read through Chapter 1 will set you up for success.

- **Start with What You Love**: Skim through the Table of Contents and mark the recipes that immediately catch your eye. Craving something sweet and creamy? Our protein ice creams will satisfy your sweet tooth. Looking for a refreshing post-workout treat.

- **Experiment with Ingredients**: Each recipe in this book is designed to be flexible. While we provide specific protein powder recommendations, feel free to experiment with what you have on hand. The same goes for fruits, nuts, and other mix-ins. This cookbook encourages creativity!

- **Nutrition at a Glance**: Health and nutrition are at the core of every recipe. At the beginning of each recipe, we provide a quick nutritional snapshot. Use this information to choose recipes that align with your dietary needs and goals.

- **Master the Basics, Then Innovate**: Once you're comfortable with a few recipes, start experimenting. Combine flavors from different recipes, adjust the sweetness, or add new textures.

- **Beyond Desserts**: Discover how the Ninja Creami can be used for more than just sweet treats. Our Beyond Desserts chapter introduces innovative ways to incorporate protein-packed frozen yogurts into your meals.

This cookbook is more than just a collection of recipes; it's a tool to help you live a healthier, more flavorful life. Each page is designed to offer you the information, inspiration, and confidence to create delicious, protein-packed treats that delight the taste buds and nourish the body. So, pre-chill your Ninja Creami bowl, stock up on your favorite protein powders, and get ready to transform the way you enjoy protein-rich desserts. Let's make something incredible together!

ABOUT THE AUTHOR

 As an advocate for health, fitness, and nutrition, Carolyn A. Bishop is deeply committed to guiding others toward vibrant lifestyles. With over a decade of experience in the industry,

Carolyn seamlessly intertwines the intricate relationships between nutrition, physical activity, and overall well-being.

Armed with a bachelor's degree in nutrition science and certified as a personal trainer, Carolyn collaborates closely with clients to craft personalized nutrition strategies tailored to their distinct needs and aspirations. Her approach goes beyond generic plans, integrating a diverse range of exercises into customized training programs to maintain client engagement and motivation.

For Carolyn, a healthy lifestyle is not just a goal but a powerful tool for both preventing and managing chronic illnesses. She emphasizes the importance of balance and moderation, empowering her clients to embrace lasting and fulfilling lifestyle changes.

Under Carolyn's guidance, clients experience remarkable transformations in their overall health and fitness levels, coupled with heightened confidence and happiness in their daily lives. Through her unwavering support and expertise, Carolyn continues to inspire individuals to embrace wellness as a way of life.

INTRODUCTION

Welcome to the "Healthy Ninja Creami Protein Cookbook," a guide dedicated to transforming the way you think about frozen treats. This book is not just a collection of recipes; it's a journey toward a healthier, more vibrant you. As someone who has always had a sweet tooth, I understand the struggle of balancing indulgence with wellness. That's where the Ninja Creami and its protein-packed frozen treats come into play, revolutionizing the concept of guilt-free desserts.

My journey with the Ninja Creami began when I was searching for a way to satisfy my cravings without compromising my health goals. Like many, I had tried various diets and fitness regimes, but the real challenge was finding a sustainable way to enjoy the frozen treats I loved. That's when I discovered the magic of the Ninja Creami. I was amazed at how this innovative machine could turn simple, wholesome ingredients into creamy, delicious treats that felt indulgent but were packed with protein and nutrients.

The Ninja Creami Protein Frozen Treats are more than just desserts; they are a testament to the power of innovation in the kitchen. With the ability to create ice cream, milkshakes, gelato, sorbet, and smoothie bowls, the Ninja Creami offers a versatile platform for experimenting with flavors and ingredients. The key principle behind these treats is simple: use protein-rich bases and natural sweeteners to create desserts that not only taste good but also fuel your body.

In today's health-conscious society, the relevance of the Ninja Creami Protein Frozen Treats cannot be overstated. We are becoming increasingly aware of the importance of protein in our diets, not just for muscle building but for overall health and wellness. These treats provide a delightful way to incorporate more protein into our daily routine, making them perfect for fitness enthusiasts, busy professionals, and families looking for nutritious snack options. What sets this cookbook apart is its unique approach to frozen treats. Each recipe is designed to be flavorful, accessible, and, most importantly, health-oriented. you'll find options that cater to your taste buds while aligning with your wellness goals.

As you set out on this culinary adventure with the "Healthy Ninja Creami Protein Cookbook," I invite you to embrace the joy of creating and savoring frozen treats that nourish your body and soul. Let this book be your guide to a world where dessert is not just a guilty pleasure but a key component of a healthy, fulfilling life.

TABLE OF CONTENT

WHAT IS NINJA CREAMI

Ninja Creami is an ice cream and frozen treat maker that can create ice cream, sorbet, milkshakes, and other treats from nearly any ingredient. Creamify is a revolutionary technology that transforms frozen solid foundations into creamy delicacies. Ninja creami is popular among individuals who adore handmade frozen desserts and want to build their tastes and textures. It comes in two versions: the 7-in-1 and the 11-in-1, each of which offers distinct functions and capacities.

Before The First Use

- To use the Ninja Creami for the first time, follow the instructions below:
- Rinse the pints, lids, and bowl with warm, soapy water and dry completely.
- Using a moist towel, wipe and dry the base and blade assembly.
- Plug in the base and power it on. The power button should light up in blue.
- Place the bowl on the base, then align the tabs. To secure it in place, twist the bowl clockwise.
- Position a pint in the bowl and line the tabs. To lock it in place, twist the pint clockwise.
- Position the blade assembly on the pint and align the tabs. To lock it in place, twist the blade assembly clockwise.
- Press the test button to ensure that everything is operating properly. The blade assembly should spin for a few seconds before stopping. If you hear strange noises or smell burning, switch off the base and call customer care.
- Turn the blade assembly, pint, and bowl counterclockwise and raise them.
- Before you introduce any ingredients into the mix, it's a good idea to do a quick test run. This is to make sure that the equipment is working perfectly. You don't need to add anything yet — just turn it on and familiarize yourself with the controls and settings.

Functions of Ninja Creami

The primary functionalities of the Ninja Creami include:

- **Ice Cream**: This function produces smooth and creamy ice cream using frozen bases like milk, cream, or yogurt.

- **Gelato**: This function produces thick and luscious gelato using frozen bases like milk, cream, or custard.

- **Sorbet**: This function makes light and delightful sorbet using frozen bases such as fruit juice, purée, or water.

- **Smoothie Bowl**: This feature makes thick, spoonable smoothie bowls from frozen bases like fruit, yogurt, or milk.

- **Milkshake**: This function makes frothy, drinkable milkshakes from frozen bases like milk, ice cream, or yogurt.

- **Re-Spin**: Smooth up a crumbly batch of ice cream with another spin or two.

Step-By-Step Processes

- Prepare your foundation mixture according to the recipe. Frozen snacks may be made using a variety of components, including milk, cream, yogurt, fruit, juice, and water.

- Pour your base mixture into the Ninja Creami pint and secure the top. Freeze the pint for 24 hours, or until absolutely solid.

- When you're ready to make your frozen treat, take the lid off the pint and set it in the Ninja Creami dish. Align the tabs and twist the pint clockwise to secure it in place.

- Place the blade assembly on top of the pint, aligning the tabs. To lock it in place, twist the blade assembly clockwise.

- Choose the function that best fits your recipe, such as Ice Cream, Gelato, Sorbet, etc. Press the start button and wait for the countdown to complete. The Ninja Creami will spin the frozen base before shaving or mixing it into a creamy dessert.

- Remove the blade assembly and pint from the bowl. Use the mix-in setting to customize your frozen delight with your toppings and extras.

- Wash the pints, lids, bowl, and blade assembly in warm, soapy water and thoroughly dry them. Wipe the base with a moist towel and let it dry.

Cleaning And Maintenance of The Ninja Creami

Cleaning and maintaining the Ninja Creami is critical to ensuring its peak performance and lifetime. Here are some recommendations for cleaning and caring for your Ninja Creami.

- After each usage, disconnect the base and allow it to cool fully.

- Rinse the pints, lids, and bowl with warm, soapy water and dry completely. Avoid using abrasive cleansers or scouring pads on these areas.

- Using a moist towel, wipe and dry the base and blade assembly. Do not submerge these components in water or place them in the dishwasher.

- Place the pints, lids, and bowl in a cold, dry location. Do not freeze or expose them to harsh temperatures.

- Regularly inspect the blade assembly for signs of wear or damage. If the blades are dull, bent, or damaged, please contact customer support for a replacement.

- Only use the Ninja Creami for preparing frozen delights. Do not use it to process hot, hard, or sticky substances. Avoid filling the cup or dish with too much base mixture or mix-ins.

Freezing Techniques for Ninja Creami

Freezing your base mixture properly is critical for creating smooth and creamy frozen delights with the Ninja Creami. Here are some freezing guidelines to follow.

- Use the Ninja Creami pints and lids included with the machine. They are intended to fit the bowl and blade assembly completely while preventing freezer burn.

- Fill the pints to the fill line and level the top of the mixture. This ensures uniform freezing and spinning.

- Freeze the pints on a flat surface in a cool freezer for at least 24 hours, or until totally solid. The freezer temperature should range from -7 to 9 degrees Fahrenheit.

- Do not freeze pints with or without lids. This is a personal preference. Some individuals prefer to freeze their ice cream without lids to prevent the hump that forms on top of it. Others like to freeze the mixture with the lids on so that it stays fresh and tidy.

- Avoid filling the pints or bowls with too much base mixture or mix-ins. This will make the spinning process more difficult and the frozen desserts less creamy.

- Do not put the quarts or dish in the freezer or expose them to high heat. This will harm the components and reduce the machine's performance.

Instructions For Safety

The Ninja Creami is a versatile machine that can make ice cream, sorbet, milkshakes, and other treats. However, it does include certain possible risks that you should be aware of and avoid. Here are some safety tips for using the Ninja Creami.

- Read all instructions before using the device and its attachments. All cautions and directions should be carefully observed and followed.

- If the appliance is left unattended, unplug it from the power supply before installing, dismantling, or cleaning.

- Before usage, thoroughly clean any components that may come into touch with food. Follow the washing directions outlined in the Quick Start Guide.

- Before each usage, check the paddle for damage. If the paddle is bent or broken, please contact customer support for a replacement.

- Do not use this equipment outside. It is intended solely for domestic home usage.

BENEFITS OF PROTEIN-RICH DESSERTS

In the world of desserts, we often find ourselves on the horns of a dilemma: the battle between the irresistible urge for a sweet treat and the commitment to eating healthily. Enter protein-rich desserts, a game-changer in how we perceive and enjoy our guilty pleasures. With the Ninja Creami Protein Cookbook, we're not just talking about any desserts; we're focusing on those that are as nourishing as they are delightful. Here's why incorporating protein-packed desserts into your diet is a brilliant move:

- **Muscle Growth and Repair**: Protein is essential for building and repairing muscles, especially after exercise. Including protein-rich meals in your diet can help maintain and increase muscle mass, which is important for overall strength and mobility.

- **Weight Management**: Protein can help you feel full for longer, reducing the likelihood of snacking on unhealthy foods. This can be particularly beneficial for those looking to manage their weight or lose excess pounds.

- **Energy Boost**: Unlike foods high in sugar that can lead to energy spikes and crashes, protein provides a more stable and sustained source of energy, helping you stay alert and focused throughout the day.

- **Bone Health**: Protein plays a crucial role in maintaining strong bones, reducing the risk of osteoporosis and bone fractures as you age.

- **Improved Metabolism**: Consuming protein can increase your metabolism, as your body uses more energy to digest protein compared to fats or carbohydrates. This can contribute to burning more calories, even at rest.

- **Better Skin, Hair, and Nails**: Protein is a building block for skin, hair, and nails. A diet rich in protein can help maintain their health and appearance, keeping your skin supple, your hair strong, and your nails less prone to breaking.

- **Immune System Support**: Protein is essential for a healthy immune system, as it helps produce antibodies and other immune cells that fight off infections and diseases.

Tips for Perfect Frozen Desserts Every Time

Whether you're wielding your Ninja Creami like a culinary wizard or just love the idea of whipping up ice cream, sorbets, and other frozen treats at home, achieving perfection every time is the dream. Here's how you can turn that dream into your everyday reality with some friendly advice:

- **Start with Quality Ingredients**: The foundation of any great dessert, frozen or not, lies in the quality of its ingredients. Fresh fruits, high-quality dairy (or dairy alternatives for the vegan adventurers), and premium protein powders not only ensure your desserts taste better but also improve their nutritional profile. Remember, better ingredients lead to a better end product.

- **Chill Your Base to the Perfect Temperature**: For those creamy concoctions that you're aiming for, starting with a well-chilled base is crucial. Make sure your mixture is cold before pouring it into your Ninja Creami container. If you're using a fruit puree or a custard base, letting it chill in the fridge for a few hours or overnight can make a world of difference.

- **Don't Overfill Your Container**: It might be tempting to maximize every batch, but overfilling your Ninja Creami container can lead to unevenly frozen desserts. Stick to the fill line to give your mixture enough space to expand and churn into that creamy texture we all love. This little bit of discipline pays off in big, delicious ways.

- **Balance Your Sweetness**: When freezing desserts, remember that cold temperatures can dull sweetness. A treat that tastes perfectly sweet at room temperature might need an extra pinch of sugar or a dash of honey to hit the same sweet spot once frozen. Taste and adjust your base accordingly before freezing.

- **Experiment with Texture**: The beauty of making your own frozen desserts is the ability to play with textures. Don't be afraid to use the Ninja Creami's various settings to find what you love. Whether it's smooth and creamy, chunky with bits of fruit or chocolate, or somewhere in between, there's a texture that's perfect for you.

- **Patience is Key**: Rushing the freezing process can lead to icy or uneven textures. Giving your dessert the full time it needs in the freezer not only ensures it's properly set but also enhances the flavor. Good things, especially in the world of frozen desserts, really do come to those who wait.

- **Clean and Maintain Your Machine**: To keep your Ninja Creami delivering perfection batch after batch, regular cleaning and maintenance are essential. Make sure to clean all parts according to the manufacturer's instructions after each use. A well-cared-for machine is the secret ingredient to consistently perfect desserts.

- **Embrace Creativity**: the most important tip: have fun with it! The Ninja Creami is your canvas, and the vast array of possible ingredients is your palette. Mix and match flavors, try out unconventional combinations, and don't be afraid to invent something new. Your next frozen masterpiece could be just a blend away.

The Basics of Protein Powders

At their core, protein powders are dietary supplements designed to provide you with a concentrated source of protein. This can come from animal sources like whey or casein, or plant sources such as peas, rice, or hemp. They're a go-to for people looking to build muscle, lose weight, or simply ensure they're getting enough protein in their diet.

Choosing the Right Protein Powder for You

Your choice of protein powder should hinge on a few key factors:

- Dietary Restrictions: Vegan, lactose intolerant, or gluten-sensitive? The protein powder is there for you.
- Taste Preferences: Chocolate, vanilla, or unflavored? The options are endless. It's worth experimenting to find your favorite.
- Nutritional Goals: Looking to bulk up, slim down, or simply maintain? Your goals can guide your choice of protein type and intake.
- Budget: Prices can vary widely, so consider how much you're willing to spend.

How to Use Protein Powder

Gone are the days of simply mixing protein powder with water. With a bit of creativity, you can incorporate protein powder into smoothies, oatmeal, baked goods, and yes, even desserts made with your Ninja Creami. The key is to start with the recommended serving size and adjust based on your dietary needs and taste preferences.

A Note on Quality: Not all protein powders are created equal. Look for brands that are transparent about their sourcing, manufacturing processes, and that provide a complete amino acid profile. Third-party testing and certification can also be a good indicator of quality.

NOTES

Fruit-Based Recipes

Tropical Paradise Milkshake

A delicious and refreshing milkshake with tropical flavors.

Ingredients:

- 1 cup frozen pineapple chunks
- 1/2 cup frozen mango chunks
- 1 banana
- 1 cup coconut milk
- 1 scoop vanilla protein powder

Prep Time: 10 minutes **Freezing Time: 24 hours** **Serving Size: 2**

Instructions:

1. In a blender, combine the pineapple, mango, banana, coconut milk, and protein powder. Blend until smooth.
2. Transfer the blended mixture into the Ninja Creami pint container. If the mixture is too thick, you can add a little more coconut milk to adjust the consistency.
3. Put the lid on the container and freeze it for at least 24 hours.
4. After it's frozen, place the container into the Ninja Creami machine.
5. Choose the 'Milkshake' option on the machine and start it.
6. Once it's done, check if it's too thick. If it is, you can use the 'Re-spin' option to mix it again.
7. Pour it into glasses and enjoy!

Nutrition Information per Serving: Calories: 280 | Total Fat: 12g (Saturated Fat: 10g, Trans Fat: 0g) | Cholesterol: 0mg | Sodium: 30mg | Protein: 8g | Carbohydrate: 38g (Dietary Fiber: 4g) | Phosphorus: 80mg | Potassium: 500mg | Calcium: 40mg

Health Benefits

- Provides energy
- Helps with muscle recovery
- Full of important nutrients

Scientific Benefits

- Pineapple and mango have special substances that help with digestion and reduce swelling.
- Coconut milk gives a type of fat that gives you energy for a longer time.

Human Experience

"I love making this milkshake after working out. It tastes like a vacation and helps me feel more awake and ready for the day."

Caution and Precaution

- Be cautious when blending frozen fruits as they can damage blender blades if too hard. Avoid over blending to retain the freshness and nutrients of the fruits.
- Ensure all fruits are thoroughly washed and properly stored before use to avoid contamination. Check for any allergies to specific fruits among consumers before serving.

Safety Measures

- Store the Tropical Paradise Milkshake in airtight containers to prevent it from absorbing odors from other foods.
- Keep the milkshake refrigerated at all times to maintain freshness and prevent bacterial growth.

Green Dream Milkshake

A nutritious and delicious milkshake packed with the goodness of greens and a hint of sweetness.

Ingredients:

- 1 cup spinach leaves
- 1/2 cup frozen avocado chunks
- 1 banana
- 1 cup almond milk

- 1 scoop vanilla protein powder
- 1 tablespoon of honey or preferred sweetener

⏲ **Prep Time: 15 minutes** ⏲ **Freezing Time: 24 hours** ◱ **Serving Size: 2**

Instructions:

1. In a blender, combine the spinach, avocado, banana, almond milk, protein powder, and sweetener. Blend until smooth.
2. Transfer the blend into the Ninja Creami pint container.
3. Place the lid on the container and freeze for at least 24 hours.
4. After freezing, insert the container into the Ninja Creami machine.
5. Select the 'Milkshake' program and start the machine.
6. Once the cycle is complete, check the consistency. If it's too thick, use the 'Re-spin' option.
7. Serve in chilled glasses and enjoy!

Nutrition Information per Serving: Calories: 220 | Total Fat: 9g (Saturated Fat: 1g, Trans Fat: 0g) | Cholesterol: 0mg | Sodium: 90mg | Protein: 10g | Carbohydrate: 28g (Dietary Fiber: 6g) | Phosphorus: 120mg | Potassium: 600mg | Calcium: 150mg

Health Benefits

- Boosts energy and vitality
- Supports digestive health
- Rich in vitamins and minerals

Scientific Benefits

- Spinach is a great source of iron, which is essential for energy production and oxygen transport in the body.
- Avocado provides healthy fats and fiber, promoting heart health and satiety.

Human Experience

"I was skeptical about green smoothies, but this milkshake changed my mind. It's delicious and makes me feel great!"

Caution and Precaution

- Take care when handling ingredients like spinach and avocado to ensure they are fresh and properly washed.
- Avoid overloading the blender with too many ingredients at once to ensure smooth blending. Check the expiration date of almond milk to ensure it is safe for consumption.
- Ensure the consistency of the milkshake is suitable for blending, adding more liquid if necessary.

Safety Measures

- Store the Green Dream Milkshake in airtight containers to prevent it from absorbing odors from other foods.
- Use opaque containers or wrap them in aluminum foil to protect the milkshake from exposure to light, which can degrade its flavor and color over time.

Berry Blast Milkshake

A vibrant and refreshing milkshake bursting with the flavors of mixed berries.

Ingredients:

- 1 cup mixed berries such as strawberries, blueberries, raspberries
- 1 banana
- 1 cup Greek yogurt
- 1 scoop vanilla protein powder
- 1 tablespoon honey or sweetener of choice

Prep Time: 10 minutes **Freezing Time: 24 hours** **Serving Size: 2**

Instructions:

1. In a blender, combine the mixed berries, banana, Greek yogurt, protein powder, and sweetener. Blend until smooth.
2. Pour the blended mixture into the Ninja Creami pint container.
3. Place the lid on the container and freeze for at least 24 hours.
4. After freezing, insert the container into the Ninja Creami machine.

5. Select the 'Milkshake' program and start the machine.

6. Once the cycle is complete, check the consistency. If it's too thick, use the 'Re-spin' option.

7. Serve in chilled glasses and enjoy!

Nutrition Information per Serving: Calories: 230 | Total Fat: 2g (Saturated Fat: 1g, Trans Fat: 0g) | Cholesterol: 10mg | Sodium: 60mg | Protein: 16g | Carbohydrate: 38g (Dietary Fiber: 4g) | Phosphorus: 150mg | Potassium: 400mg | Calcium: 150mg

Health Benefits

- Boosts immune system
- Rich in antioxidants
- Supports digestive health

Scientific Benefits

- Berries are high in antioxidants, which can help protect the body from free radical damage.
- Greek yogurt offers probiotics, aiding in maintaining gut health and promoting digestion.

Human Experience

"This milkshake is like a burst of summer in a glass. It's so refreshing and keeps me feeling light and energized."

Caution & Precaution

- Be cautious when blending frozen berries to prevent damaging the blender blades.
- Ensure all berries are properly washed and checked for any signs of spoilage before use.

Safety Measures

- Store the Berry Blast Milkshake in airtight containers to prevent absorption of odors from other foods.
- Refrigerate the milkshake promptly and keep it chilled at all times to maintain freshness and prevent bacterial growth.

Pumpkin Spice Protein Delight Milkshake

A creamy and spiced milkshake that captures the essence of fall with pumpkin and warm spices.

Ingredients:

- 1 cup pumpkin puree
- 1 cup milk of choice
- 1 scoop vanilla protein powder
- 1 teaspoon pumpkin pie spice
- 1 tablespoon of maple syrup or preferred sweetener

⏲ **Prep Time: 30 minutes** ⏲ **Freezing Time: 24 hours** 🍽 **Serving Size: 2**

Instructions:

1. In a blender, combine the pumpkin puree, milk, protein powder, pumpkin pie spice, and sweetener. Blend until smooth.
2. Transfer the blended mixture into the Ninja Creami pint container.
3. Place the lid on the container and freeze for at least 24 hours.
4. After freezing, insert the container into the Ninja Creami machine.
5. Select the 'Milkshake' program and start the machine.
6. Once the cycle is complete, check the consistency. If it's too thick, use the 'Re-spin' option.
7. Serve in chilled glasses and enjoy!

Nutrition Information per Serving: Calories: 180 | Total Fat: 3g (Saturated Fat: 1g, Trans Fat: 0g) | Cholesterol: 15mg | Sodium: 80mg | Protein: 15g | Carbohydrate: 24g (Dietary Fiber: 3g) | Phosphorus: 150mg | Potassium: 300mg | Calcium: 200mg

Health Benefits:

- Boosts immunity
- Supports digestion
- Rich in vitamins and minerals

Scientific Benefits

- Pumpkin is a great source of beta-carotene, which is converted to vitamin A in the body and supports immune function.
- The spices used in pumpkin pie spice, such as cinnamon and nutmeg, have anti-inflammatory properties.

Human Experience

"This milkshake is my favorite way to enjoy the flavors of fall. It's comforting, satisfying, and gives me a great protein boost."

Caution & Precaution

- Avoid adding too much pumpkin pie spice to prevent overpowering the flavor.
- Adjust the consistency of the milkshake by adding more or less liquid as needed.

Safety Measures

- Store the Pumpkin Spice Protein Delight Milkshake in airtight containers to preserve its flavor and prevent contamination.
- Keep the milkshake refrigerated to maintain its freshness and prevent spoilage, especially due to the inclusion of perishable ingredients like pumpkin puree.

Carrot Cake Crusher Milkshake

A delicious and healthy milkshake that tastes just like a slice of carrot cake.

Ingredients:

- 1 cup grated carrots
- 1 cup almond milk
- 1 scoop vanilla protein powder
- 1/2 teaspoon cinnamon
- 1/4 teaspoon nutmeg
- 1 tablespoon of maple syrup or preferred sweetener

Prep Time: 15 minutes **Freezing Time: 24 hours** **Serving Size: 2**

Instructions:

1. In a blender, combine the grated carrots, almond milk, protein powder, cinnamon, nutmeg, and sweetener. Blend until smooth.
2. Transfer the blended mixture into the Ninja Creami pint container
3. Place the lid on the container and freeze for at least 24 hours.
4. After freezing, insert the container into the Ninja Creami machine.
5. Select the 'Milkshake' program and start the machine.
6. Once the cycle is complete, check the consistency. If it's too thick, use the 'Re-spin' option.
7. Serve in chilled glasses and enjoy!

Nutrition Information per Serving: Calories: 160 | Total Fat: 2g (Saturated Fat: 0g, Trans Fat: 0g) | Cholesterol: 0mg | Sodium: 150mg | Protein: 15g | Carbohydrate: 22g (Dietary Fiber: 3g) | Phosphorus: 100mg | Potassium: 350mg | Calcium: 200mg

Health Benefits

- Supports eye health
- Boosts immune system
- Rich in fiber and antioxidants

Scientific Benefits

- Carrots are high in beta-carotene, which is important for vision and immune function.
- Cinnamon and nutmeg have anti-inflammatory and antioxidant properties.

Human Experience

"This milkshake is a game-changer for me. It satisfies my sweet cravings while still being nutritious. Plus, it's so easy to make!"

Caution and Precaution

- Handle the blender with care to prevent spills and ensure proper blending consistency.
- Ensure all ingredients are properly blended to avoid any chunks that may affect the texture of the milkshake.

Safety Measures

- Store the Carrot Cake Crusher Milkshake in glass jars with tight-fitting lids to prevent air exposure and maintain freshness.
- Place the milkshake jars on a shelf away from the refrigerator door to minimize temperature fluctuations and ensure consistent cooling.

Chocolate-Based Recipes

Mocha Madness Milkshake

A rich and creamy milkshake that combines the bold flavors of coffee and chocolate.

Ingredients:

- 1 cup strong brewed coffee, cooled
- 1/2 cup milk of choice
- 1 scoop chocolate protein powder
- 2 tablespoons cocoa powder
- 1 tablespoon of honey or Preferred sweetener

Prep Time: 10 minutes **Freezing Time: 24 hours** **Serving Size: 2**

Instructions:

1. In a blender, combine the brewed coffee, milk, chocolate protein powder, cocoa powder, and sweetener. Blend until smooth.
2. Transfer the blended mixture into the Ninja Creami pint container.
3. Place the lid on the container and freeze for at least 24 hours.
4. After freezing, insert the container into the Ninja Creami machine.
5. Select the 'Milkshake' program and start the machine.
6. Once the cycle is complete, check the consistency. If it's too thick, use the 'Re-spin' option.
7. Serve in chilled glasses and enjoy!

Nutrition Information per Serving: Calories: 180 | Total Fat: 3g (Saturated Fat: 1g, Trans Fat: 0g) | Cholesterol: 15mg | Sodium: 80mg | Protein: 15g | Carbohydrate: 24g (Dietary Fiber: 3g) | Phosphorus: 150mg | Potassium: 400mg | Calcium: 100mg

Health Benefits

- Boosts energy and focus
- Supports muscle recovery
- Rich in antioxidants

Scientific Benefits

- Coffee includes caffeine, a substance known to enhance both cognitive alertness and physical capabilities..
- Cocoa powder is rich in flavonoids, which have been linked to heart health and reduced inflammation.

Human Experience

"This milkshake is my go-to for busy mornings. It gives me the energy I need to start my day, and the chocolate flavor satisfies my sweet tooth."

Caution & Precaution

- Use caution when handling hot brewed coffee to prevent burns.
- Be mindful of the caffeine content in the milkshake, especially when serving to individuals sensitive to caffeine.

Safety Measures

- Store the Mocha Madness Milkshake in airtight containers to preserve its flavor and prevent contamination.

Chocolate Cherry Jubilee Milkshake

A decadent and rich milkshake that combines the classic flavors of chocolate and cherries.

Ingredients:

- 1 cup frozen cherries
- 1 cup milk of choice
- 1 scoop chocolate protein powder
- 2 tablespoons cocoa powder

- 1 tablespoon of honey or preferred sweetener of choice

⏲ **Prep Time: 15 minutes** ⏲ **Freezing Time: 24 hours** 🍽 **Serving Size: 2**

Instructions:

1. In a blender, combine the frozen cherries, milk, chocolate protein powder, cocoa powder, and sweetener. Blend until smooth.
2. Transfer the blended mixture into the Ninja Creami pint container.
3. Place the lid on the container and freeze for at least 24 hours.
4. After freezing, insert the container into the Ninja Creami machine.
5. Select the 'Milkshake' program and start the machine.
6. Once the cycle is complete, check the consistency. If it's too thick, use the 'Re-spin' option.
7. Serve in chilled glasses and enjoy!

Nutrition Information per Serving: Calories: 200 | Total Fat: 3g (Saturated Fat: 1g, Trans Fat: 0g) | Cholesterol: 10mg | Sodium: 80mg | Protein: 15g | Carbohydrate: 30g (Dietary Fiber: 4g) | Phosphorus: 150mg | Potassium: 400mg | Calcium: 150mg

Health Benefits

- Rich in antioxidants
- Supports muscle recovery
- Promotes heart health

Scientific Benefits

- Cherries are known for their high antioxidant content, which can help reduce inflammation and protect against chronic diseases.
- Cocoa powder contains flavonoids that are beneficial for heart health.

Human Experience

"I'm a huge fan of this milkshake. It's like having dessert, but it's actually good for you. It's a treat I don't feel guilty about indulging in."

Caution and Precaution

- Handle frozen cherries carefully to prevent damage to blender blades.
- Ensure all ingredients are properly measured and blended evenly to achieve a smooth consistency.

Safety Measures

- Store the Chocolate Cherry Jubilee Milkshake in airtight containers to preserve its flavor and prevent contamination.
- Keep the milkshake refrigerated to maintain its freshness and prevent spoilage, especially due to the inclusion of perishable ingredients like cherries.

Cookies & Cream Craze Milkshake

A classic and indulgent milkshake that perfectly captures the beloved cookies and cream flavor.

Ingredients:

- 1 cup milk of choice
- 1 scoop vanilla protein powder
- 3 chocolate sandwich cookies, crushed
- 1 tablespoon of honey or preferred sweetener of choice

Prep Time: 10 minutes **Freezing Time: 24 hours** **Serving Size: 2**

Instructions:

1. In a blender, combine the milk, protein powder, crushed cookies, and sweetener. Blend until smooth.
2. Transfer the blended mixture into the Ninja Creami pint container.
3. Place the lid on the container and freeze for at least 24 hours.
4. After freezing, insert the container into the Ninja Creami machine.
5. Select the 'Milkshake' program and start the machine.
6. Once the cycle is complete, check the consistency. If it's too thick, use the 'Re-spin' option.
7. Serve in chilled glasses and enjoy!

Nutrition Information per Serving: Calories: 220 | Total Fat: 7g (Saturated Fat: 3g, Trans Fat: 0g) | Cholesterol: 10mg | Sodium: 200mg | Protein: 15g | Carbohydrate: 28g (Dietary Fiber: 1g) | Phosphorus: 150mg | Potassium: 300mg | Calcium: 200mg

Health Benefits

- Provides a protein boost
- Satisfies sweet cravings in a healthier way
- Can be made with alternative milks for dietary needs

Scientific Benefits

- Protein supports muscle repair and growth, making this milkshake a great post-workout treat.
- Using alternative milks like almond or soy can provide additional health benefits such as lower cholesterol levels.

Human Experience

"This milkshake is my guilty pleasure. It's so creamy and delicious, and I love that I can enjoy it without feeling like I'm cheating on my diet."

Caution & Precaution

- Ensure that the cookies are crushed evenly to achieve a consistent texture throughout the milkshake.
- Confirm any allergies to chocolate or cookies among consumers before serving.

Safety Measures

- Store the Cookies & Cream Craze Milkshake containers away from strong-smelling foods in the refrigerator to prevent flavor absorption and maintain the milkshake's distinct taste.
- Position the milkshake containers upright in the refrigerator to prevent potential leaks or spills that could contaminate other food items stored nearby.

Nut-Based Recipe

Peanut Butter Powerhouse Milkshake

A creamy and indulgent milkshake that's packed with protein and the rich flavor of peanut butter.

Ingredients:

- 1 cup milk of choice
- 1/4 cup natural peanut butter
- 1 banana
- 1 scoop vanilla protein powder
- 1 tablespoon of honey or preferred sweetener of choice

Prep Time: 10 minutes ⏰ **Freezing Time: 24 hours** **Serving Size: 2**

Instructions:

1. In a blender, combine the milk, peanut butter, banana, protein powder, and sweetener. Blend until smooth.
2. Transfer the mixture into the Ninja Creami pint container.
3. Place the lid on the container and freeze for at least 24 hours.
4. After freezing, insert the container into the Ninja Creami machine.
5. Select the 'Milkshake' program and start the machine.
6. Once the cycle is complete, check the consistency. If it's too thick, use the 'Re-spin' option.
7. Serve in chilled glasses and enjoy!

Nutrition Information per Serving: Calories: 320 | Total Fat: 16g (Saturated Fat: 3g, Trans Fat: 0g) | Cholesterol: 10mg | Sodium: 150mg | Protein: 18g | Carbohydrate: 28g (Dietary Fiber: 4g) | Phosphorus: 200mg | Potassium: 500mg | Calcium: 200mg

Health Benefits

- Provides sustained energy
- Supports muscle growth and repair
- Rich in healthy fats and protein

Scientific Benefits

- Peanut butter is a good source of monounsaturated fats, which are beneficial for heart health.
- Protein helps in muscle synthesis and repair, making this milkshake ideal for post-workout recovery.

Human Experience

This milkshake is an essential part of my fitness regimen. It's not only delicious but also keeps me full and energized after my workouts."

Caution and Precaution

- Exercise caution when blending peanut butter to avoid clumping and ensure smooth consistency. Be mindful of peanut allergies among consumers before serving

- Ensure proper cleaning of blender components due to potential allergen cross-contamination.

Safety Measures

- Store the Peanut Butter Powerhouse Milkshake in airtight containers to prevent contamination and preserve its flavor.

- Keep the milkshake refrigerated to maintain freshness and prevent spoilage, especially due to the inclusion of perishable ingredients like milk and banana.

Unique flavor Combination Recipe

Matcha Mint Marvel Milkshake

A refreshing and energizing milkshake that combines the unique flavor of matcha with a hint of mint.

Ingredients:

- 1 cup almond milk
- 1 scoop vanilla protein powder
- 1 teaspoon matcha green tea powder
- 1/4 cup fresh mint leaves
- 1 tablespoon of honey or preferred sweetener of choice

Prep Time: 15 minutes Freezing Time: 24 hours Serving Size: 2

Instructions:

1. In a blender, combine the almond milk, protein powder, matcha powder, mint leaves, and sweetener. Blend until smooth.

2. Transfer the blended mixture into the Ninja Creami pint container. Place the lid on the container and freeze for at least 24 hours.

3. After freezing, insert the container into the Ninja Creami machine.

4. Select the 'Milkshake' program and start the machine.

5. Once the cycle is complete, check the consistency. If it's too thick, use the 'Re-spin' option.

6. Serve in chilled glasses and enjoy!

Nutrition Information per Serving: Calories: 130 | Total Fat: 3g (Saturated Fat: 0g, Trans Fat: 0g) | Cholesterol: 0mg | Sodium: 150mg | Protein: 15g | Carbohydrate: 14g (Dietary Fiber: 2g) | Phosphorus: 100mg | Potassium: 200mg | Calcium: 150mg

Health Benefits

- Boosts metabolism and rich in antioxidants

Scientific Benefits

- Matcha is high in catechins, which are antioxidants that can help prevent cell damage and reduce inflammation. Mint has been shown to aid in digestion and provide a natural energy boost.

Human Experience

"I love starting my day with this milkshake. The matcha and mint combination is so invigorating, and it keeps me focused and energized throughout the morning."

Caution & Precaution

- Use caution when handling matcha powder to avoid inhaling it, as it can be irritating to the lungs.
- Too much matcha can make the milkshake bitter.

Safety Measures

- Not recommended, Matcha loses its vibrant color and flavor over time, and the milkshake will separate

Fruit-Based Recipes

Strawberry Cheesecake Delight

A creamy and fruity ice cream that captures the essence of a classic strawberry cheesecake.

Ingredients:

- 2 cups heavy cream
- 1 cup whole milk
- 3/4 cup granulated sugar
- 1 scoop vanilla protein powder
- 1 teaspoon vanilla extract
- 1/2 cup cream cheese, softened
- 1/2 cup strawberry puree
- 1/2 cup graham cracker crumbs

Prep Time: 20 minutes   **Freezing Time: 24 hours**   **Serving Size: 4**

Instructions:

1. In a blender, combine the heavy cream, milk, sugar, protein powder, vanilla extract, and cream cheese. Blend until smooth.
2. Transfer the blended mixture into the Ninja Creami pint container. Add the strawberry puree and graham cracker crumbs, and mix gently to distribute evenly.
3. Place the lid on the container and freeze for at least 24 hours.
4. After freezing, insert the container into the Ninja Creami machine.
5. Select the 'Ice Cream' program and start the machine.
6. Once the cycle is complete, check the consistency. If it's too thick, use the 'Re-spin' option.
7. Serve in bowls and enjoy the Strawberry Cheesecake Delight!

Nutrition Information per Serving: Calories: 450 | Total Fat: 32g (Saturated Fat: 20g, Trans Fat: 0g) | Cholesterol: 120mg | Sodium: 220mg | Protein: 9g | Carbohydrate: 36g (Dietary Fiber: 1g) | Phosphorus: 140mg | Potassium: 200mg | Calcium: 190mg

Health Benefits

- Strawberries offer a valuable supply of protein and calcium.
- Additionally, they are abundant in antioxidants and vitamin C, providing essential nutrients for overall health.

Scientific Benefits

- Cream cheese contains probiotics that can support gut health
- Strawberries have been linked to heart health and improved blood sugar control

Human Experience

"This ice cream is a hit at every family gathering. It's so creamy and has the perfect balance of sweetness and tanginess."

Caution and Precaution

- Avoid overmixing the strawberry puree into the ice cream mixture to maintain a swirl-like appearance.
- Ensure the cream cheese is softened properly to avoid lumps in the ice cream.

Safety Measures

- Store the ice cream in a sealed container in the coldest part of the freezer to prevent the formation of ice crystals.
- Use pasteurized eggs or egg substitutes in the recipe to reduce the risk of foodborne illness.

Blackberry Lavender Bliss

A refreshing and floral ice cream that pairs the sweet-tart flavor of blackberries with the soothing aroma of lavender.

Ingredients:

- 2 cups heavy cream

- 1 cup whole milk
- 3/4 cup blackberry puree
- 1 scoop vanilla protein powder
- 1 tablespoon dried lavender flowers
- 1/2 cup granulated sugar

⏱ **Prep Time: 15 minutes** ⏱ **Freezing Time: 24 hours** 🍽 **Serving Size: 4**

Instructions:

1. In a blender, combine the heavy cream, milk, blackberry puree, protein powder, lavender flowers, and sugar. Blend until smooth.
2. Transfer the mixture into the Ninja Creami pint container.
3. Place the lid on the container and freeze for at least 24 hours.
4. After freezing, insert the container into the Ninja Creami machine.
5. Select the 'Ice Cream' program and start the machine.
6. Once the cycle is complete, check the consistency. If it's too thick, use the 'Re-spin' option.
7. Serve in bowls and enjoy the Blackberry Lavender Bliss!

Nutrition Information per Serving: Calories: 370 | Total Fat: 26g (Saturated Fat: 16g, Trans Fat: 0g) | Cholesterol: 95mg | Sodium: 60mg | Protein: 8g | Carbohydrate: 30g (Dietary Fiber: 1g) | Phosphorus: 140mg | Potassium: 200mg | Calcium: 180mg

Health Benefits
- Provides a good source of antioxidants and protein
- Lavender is known for its calming properties

Human Experience
"The Blackberry Lavender Bliss ice cream is like a taste of summer. It's so refreshing, and the lavender adds a unique and relaxing touch."

Caution and Precaution
- Be cautious when blending the lavender flowers to avoid overprocessing, which can lead to a bitter taste.

- Strain the blackberry puree before adding it to the ice cream mixture to remove any seeds or pulp.

Safety Measures

- Label the container with the date the ice cream was made to ensure it is consumed within a reasonable time frame.
- Clean and sanitize all equipment thoroughly before use to prevent cross-contamination of ingredients.

Blueberry Muffin Magic

A delightful ice cream that captures the essence of a freshly baked blueberry muffin, complete with bursts of blueberries and a hint of cinnamon.

Ingredients:

- 2 cups heavy cream
- 1 cup whole milk
- 3/4 cup granulated sugar
- 1 scoop vanilla protein powder
- 1/2 teaspoon ground cinnamon
- 1 cup fresh or frozen blueberries
- 1/2 cup streusel topping or crumbled muffin pieces

Prep Time: 15 minutes **Freezing Time: 24 hours** **Serving Size: 4**

Instructions:

- In a blender, combine the heavy cream, milk, sugar, protein powder, and cinnamon. Blend until smooth.
- Transfer the mixture into the Ninja Creami pint container. Add the blueberries and streusel topping or crumbled muffin pieces, and mix gently to distribute evenly.
- Place the lid on the container and freeze for at least 24 hours.
- After freezing, insert the container into the Ninja Creami machine.
- Select the 'Ice Cream' program and start the machine.
- Once the cycle is complete, check the consistency. If it's too thick, use the 'Re-spin' option.

- Serve in bowls and enjoy the Blueberry Muffin Magic!

Nutrition Information per Serving: Calories: 420 | Total Fat: 28g (Saturated Fat: 18g, Trans Fat: 0g) | Cholesterol: 110mg | Sodium: 120mg | Protein: 8g | Carbohydrate: 38g (Dietary Fiber: 2g) | Phosphorus: 130mg | Potassium: 200mg | Calcium: 180mg

Health Benefits

- Provides a good source of protein and antioxidants
- Blueberries are known for their health benefits, including supporting heart health and cognitive function

Human Experience

"The Blueberry Muffin Magic ice cream is like having breakfast for dessert. It's so flavorful and comforting, and I love the texture of the streusel topping."

Caution and Precaution

- Ensure the streusel topping or crumbled muffin pieces are dry to prevent them from becoming soggy when mixed into the ice cream.
- Use fresh or properly thawed frozen blueberries to maintain the texture and flavor of the ice cream.

Safety Measures:

- Store the ice cream away from strong-smelling foods in the freezer to prevent flavor contamination.
- When serving, use a clean utensil to scoop out the ice cream to avoid cross-contamination.

Chocolate-Based Recipes

Chocolate Chip Cookie Dough Dream

A decadent ice cream packed with chunks of chocolate chip cookie dough and a rich, creamy base.

Ingredients:

- 2 cups heavy cream
- 1 cup whole milk

- 3/4 cup brown sugar

- 1 scoop vanilla protein powder

- 1 teaspoon vanilla extract

- 1/2 cup chocolate chip cookie dough, chopped into small pieces

⏱ **Prep Time: 15 minutes** ⏱ **Freezing Time: 24 hours** 🍽 **Serving Size: 4**

Instructions:

1. In a blender, combine the heavy cream, milk, brown sugar, protein powder, and vanilla extract. Blend until smooth.

2. Transfer the mixture into the Ninja Creami pint container. Add the chopped cookie dough pieces and mix gently to distribute evenly.

3. Place the lid on the container and freeze for at least 24 hours.

4. After freezing, insert the container into the Ninja Creami machine.

5. Select the 'Ice Cream' program and start the machine.

6. Once the cycle is complete, check the consistency. If it's too thick, use the 'Re-spin' option.

7. Serve in bowls and enjoy the Chocolate Chip Cookie Dough Dream!

Nutrition Information per Serving: Calories: 400 | Total Fat: 28g (Saturated Fat: 18g, Trans Fat: 0g) | Cholesterol: 100mg | Sodium: 80mg | Protein: 8g | Carbohydrate: 34g (Dietary Fiber: 0g) | Phosphorus: 120mg | Potassium: 180mg | Calcium: 170mg

Health Benefits

- Offers a rich source of protein and calcium.

- Can be a satisfying treat in moderation.

Scientific Benefits

- Protein supports muscle repair and growth

- Calcium is essential for bone health

Human Experience

" This frozen treat is a delightful indulgence for those who adore cookie dough! It's so rich and satisfying, perfect for indulging in a sweet craving."

Caution and Precaution

- Chop the cookie dough into small, uniform pieces to prevent them from jamming the blender blades.
- Ensure the ice cream mixture is completely frozen before churning to achieve the desired consistency.

Safety Measures

- Store the ice cream in a shallow container to facilitate quicker freezing and minimize the formation of large ice crystals.

S'mores Sensation

A nostalgic ice cream that brings together the classic flavors of s'mores - chocolate, marshmallows, and graham crackers.

Ingredients:

- 2 cups heavy cream
- 1 cup whole milk
- 3/4 cup granulated sugar
- 1 scoop vanilla protein powder
- 1/2 cup chocolate chips
- 1/2 cup mini marshmallows
- 1/2 cup crushed graham crackers

⏲ Prep Time: 10 minutes ⏲ Freezing Time: 24 hours 🍽 Serving Size: 4

Instructions:

1. In a blender, combine the heavy cream, milk, sugar, and protein powder. Blend until smooth.
2. Transfer the mixture into the Ninja Creami pint container. Add the chocolate chips, mini marshmallows, and crushed graham crackers, and mix gently to distribute evenly.
3. Place the lid on the container and freeze for at least 24 hours.
4. After freezing, insert the container into the Ninja Creami machine.

5. Select the 'Ice Cream' program and start the machine.

6. Once the cycle is complete, check the consistency. If it's too thick, use the 'Re-spin' option.

7. Serve in bowls and enjoy the S'mores Sensation!

Nutrition Information per Serving: Calories: 420 | Total Fat: 28g (Saturated Fat: 18g, Trans Fat: 0g) | Cholesterol: 110mg | Sodium: 180mg | Protein: 8g | Carbohydrate: 38g (Dietary Fiber: 1g) | Phosphorus: 130mg | Potassium: 190mg | Calcium: 180mg

Health Benefits

- Provides a good source of protein
- Can be a fun and indulgent treat for special occasions

Human Experience

"The S'mores Sensation ice cream is like a campfire in a bowl. It's so comforting and delicious, and it brings back great memories of summer nights."

Caution and Precaution

- Be careful when adding the chocolate chips to the ice cream mixture to avoid splashing or spilling.
- Crush the graham crackers into small pieces to ensure they are evenly distributed throughout the ice cream.

Safety Measures

- Keep the ice cream machine and surrounding area dry to prevent slips and falls during the churning process.
- Store the ice cream away from strong-smelling foods in the freezer to prevent flavor transfer.

Nut-Based Recipes

Pistachio Paradise

A nutty and luxurious ice cream that's infused with the rich flavor of pistachios for a unique and indulgent treat.

Ingredients:

- 2 cups heavy cream
- 1 cup whole milk
- 3/4 cup granulated sugar
- 1 scoop vanilla protein powder
- 1 teaspoon almond extract
- 1/2 cup pistachios, finely chopped

⏱ **Prep Time: 10 minutes** ⏱ **Freezing Time: 24 hours** 🍽 **Serving Size: 4**

Instructions:

1. In a blender, combine the heavy cream, milk, sugar, protein powder, and almond extract. Blend until smooth. Add a few drops of green food coloring if desired for a more vibrant color.
2. Transfer the mixture into the Ninja Creami pint container. Add the chopped pistachios and mix gently to distribute evenly.
3. Place the lid on the container and freeze for at least 24 hours.
4. After freezing, insert the container into the Ninja Creami machine.
5. Select the 'Ice Cream' program and start the machine.
6. Once the cycle is complete, check the consistency. If it's too thick, use the 'Re-spin' option.
7. Serve in bowls and enjoy the Pistachio Paradise!

Nutrition Information per Serving: Calories: 370 | Total Fat: 26g (Saturated Fat: 15g, Trans Fat: 0g) | Cholesterol: 95mg | Sodium: 70mg | Protein: 9g | Carbohydrate: 28g (Dietary Fiber: 1g) | Phosphorus: 160mg | Potassium: 230mg | Calcium: 180mg

Health Benefits

- Provides a good source of protein and healthy fats
- Pistachios are rich in antioxidants and have heart-healthy benefits

Scientific Benefits

- Pistachios contain healthy fats, fiber, and protein, which can help with satiety and weight management

- Almond extract contains compounds that have been linked to improved mood and cognitive function

Human Experience

" My top pick for ice cream flavor is definitely Pistachio Paradise. It's so rich and flavorful, and I love the crunch from the pistachios."

Caution and Precaution

- Check for any shell remnants in the chopped pistachios to prevent potential choking hazards.
- Use natural pistachios without added artificial colors to maintain the authentic flavor and appearance of the ice cream.

Safety Measures

- Store the ice cream away from other products containing nuts to prevent cross-contamination and allergen exposure.
- When serving, inform individuals with nut allergies about the ingredients and potential risks.

Salted Caramel Pretzel

A decadent ice cream that combines the sweet and salty flavors of salted caramel with the crunchy texture of pretzels.

Ingredients:

- 2 cups heavy cream
- 1 cup whole milk
- 3/4 cup caramel sauce
- 1 scoop vanilla protein powder
- 1/2 teaspoon sea salt
- 1/2 cup crushed pretzels

Prep Time: 10 minutes   **Freezing Time: 24 hours**   **Serving Size: 4**

Instructions:

1. In a blender, combine the heavy cream, milk, caramel sauce, protein powder, and sea salt. Blend until smooth.

2. Transfer the mixture into the Ninja Creami pint container. Add the crushed pretzels and mix gently to distribute evenly.

3. Place the lid on the container and freeze for at least 24 hours.

4. After freezing, insert the container into the Ninja Creami machine.

5. Select the 'Ice Cream' program and start the machine.

6. Once the cycle is complete, check the consistency. If it's too thick, use the 'Re-spin' option.

7. Serve in bowls and enjoy the Salted Caramel Pretzel Party!

Nutrition Information per Serving: Calories: 400 | Total Fat: 28g (Saturated Fat: 18g, Trans Fat: 0g) | Cholesterol: 100mg | Sodium: 350mg | Protein: 8g | Carbohydrate: 34g (Dietary Fiber: 0g) | Phosphorus: 120mg | Potassium: 180mg | Calcium: 170mg

Health Benefits

- Provides a good source of protein
- Can satisfy sweet and salty cravings in moderation

Human Experience

"This ice cream is the perfect combination of sweet and salty. The crunchy pretzels add a fun twist that I can't get enough of!"

Caution and Precaution

- Monitor the caramel sauce closely while heating to prevent it from burning and becoming bitter.
- Precaution: Crush the pretzels into small pieces to avoid damaging the blender blades when mixing.

Safety Measures

- Avoid refreezing melted ice cream to maintain its texture and quality.
- Keep the ice cream scoop clean and dry to prevent cross-contamination when serving.

Coffee Almond Crunch

A rich and robust ice cream that combines the bold flavor of coffee with the crunch of almonds for a satisfying texture.

Ingredients:

- 2 cups heavy cream
- 1 cup whole milk
- 3/4 cup brewed espresso, cooled
- 1 scoop vanilla protein powder
- 1/2 cup granulated sugar
- 1/2 cup roasted almonds, chopped

Prep Time: 15 minutes   Freezing Time: 24 hours   Serving Size: 4

Instructions:

1. In a blender, combine the heavy cream, milk, espresso, protein powder, and sugar. Blend until smooth.
2. Transfer the mixture into the Ninja Creami pint container. Add the chopped almonds and mix gently to distribute evenly.
3. Place the lid on the container and freeze for at least 24 hours.
4. After freezing, insert the container into the Ninja Creami machine.
5. Select the 'Ice Cream' program and start the machine.
6. Once the cycle is complete, check the consistency. If it's too thick, use the 'Re-spin' option.
7. Serve in bowls and enjoy the Coffee Almond Crunch!

Nutrition Information per Serving: Calories: 380 | Total Fat: 28g (Saturated Fat: 16g, Trans Fat: 0g) | Cholesterol: 95mg | Sodium: 70mg | Protein: 9g | Carbohydrate: 28g (Dietary Fiber: 1g) | Phosphorus: 160mg | Potassium: 220mg | Calcium: 190mg

Health Benefits

- Provides a good source of protein and healthy fats
- Coffee is known for its antioxidant properties and can boost energy levels

Human Experience

"I often turn to the Coffee Almond Crunch ice cream for a quick energy boost. It's the perfect combination of flavors and textures."

Caution and Precaution

- Be cautious with the amount of brewed espresso added to avoid overpowering the flavor of the ice cream with bitterness.
- Use roasted almonds that are free from any added salt or seasoning to control the overall sodium content of the ice cream.

Safety Measures

- Store the ice cream away from strong-smelling foods in the freezer to prevent absorption of odors.
- Ensure the ice cream scoop used for serving is clean and sanitized to maintain food safety.

Snickerdoodle Surprise

A creamy and cinnamon-spiced ice cream that captures the essence of the classic Snickerdoodle cookie, with a delightful surprise of cinnamon sugar swirls throughout.

Ingredients:

- 2 cups heavy cream
- 1 cup whole milk
- 3/4 cup granulated sugar
- 1 scoop vanilla protein powder
- 2 teaspoons ground cinnamon
- 1 teaspoon vanilla extract
- 1/2 cup cinnamon sugar swirl (mix 1/4 cup sugar with 1 tablespoon cinnamon)

Prep Time: 12 minutes **Freezing Time: 24 hours** **Serving Size: 4**

Instructions:

1. In a blender, combine the heavy cream, milk, granulated sugar, protein powder, ground cinnamon, and vanilla extract. Blend until smooth.

2. Transfer the mixture into the Ninja Creami pint container. Swirl in the cinnamon sugar mixture, but do not mix completely; aim for a marbled effect.

3. Place the lid on the container and freeze for at least 24 hours.

4. After freezing, insert the container into the Ninja Creami machine.

5. Select the 'Ice Cream' program and start the machine.

6. Once the cycle is complete, check the consistency. If it's too thick, use the 'Re-spin' option.

7. Serve in bowls and enjoy the Snickerdoodle Surprise with its delightful cinnamon sugar swirls!

Nutrition Information per Serving: Calories: 420 | Total Fat: 28g (Saturated Fat: 18g, Trans Fat: 0g) | Cholesterol: 110mg | Sodium: 85mg | Protein: 8g | Carbohydrate: 38g (Dietary Fiber: 0g) | Phosphorus: 130mg | Potassium: 190mg | Calcium: 180mg

Health Benefits

- It offers a rich source of protein and calcium.
- Cinnamon has anti-inflammatory properties which boost and aids in balancing blood sugar levels.

Human Experience

"The Snickerdoodle Surprise ice cream is incredible! The cinnamon sugar swirls add such a fun and tasty twist. It's like enjoying my favorite cookie in ice cream form."

Caution and Precaution

- Incorporate the cinnamon sugar swirl gently to create a marbled effect without fully mixing it into the ice cream.
- Adjust the amount of cinnamon sugar swirl added to achieve the desired level of sweetness and cinnamon flavor.

Safety Measures

- Store the ice cream in a tightly sealed container to prevent freezer burn and maintain freshness.
- Use caution when consuming if anyone has a known cinnamon allergy, and clearly label the container accordingly.

Birthday Cake Bash

A celebratory ice cream that captures the fun and sweetness of a classic birthday cake, complete with sprinkles and a vanilla cake flavor.

Ingredients

- 2 cups heavy cream
- 1 cup whole milk
- 3/4 cup granulated sugar
- 1 scoop vanilla protein powder
- 1 teaspoon vanilla extract
- 1/2 cup rainbow sprinkles
- 1/2 cup yellow cake mix

Prep Time: 10 minutes **Freezing Time: 24 hours** **Serving Size: 4**

Instructions

1. In a blender, combine the heavy cream, milk, sugar, protein powder, vanilla extract, and yellow cake mix. Blend until smooth.
2. Transfer the mixture into the Ninja Creami pint container. Add the rainbow sprinkles and mix gently to distribute evenly.
3. Place the lid on the container and freeze for at least 24 hours.
4. After freezing, insert the container into the Ninja Creami machine.
5. Select the 'Ice Cream' program and start the machine.
6. Once the cycle is complete, check the consistency. If it's too thick, use the 'Re-spin' option.
7. Serve in bowls and enjoy the Birthday Cake Bash!

Nutrition Information per Serving: Calories: 420 | Total Fat: 28g (Saturated Fat: 18g, Trans Fat: 0g) | Cholesterol: 110mg | Sodium: 180mg | Protein: 8g | Carbohydrate: 38g (Dietary Fiber: 0g) | Phosphorus: 130mg | Potassium: 190mg | Calcium: 180mg

Health Benefits

- Provides a good source of protein
- Can be a fun and festive treat for special occasions

Human Experience

"This ice cream is like having a birthday party in a bowl. It's so colorful and delicious, and it brings back great memories!"

Caution and Precaution

- Avoid overmixing the rainbow sprinkles into the ice cream mixture to prevent the colors from bleeding excessively.
- Use a high-quality yellow cake mix to ensure the ice cream has a rich and authentic birthday cake flavor.

Safety Measures

- Store the ice cream in a designated section of the freezer away from raw foods to prevent contamination.
- When serving, ensure the bowls or cones are clean and free from any debris or contaminants.

Fruit-Based Recipes

Berry Protein Power Bowl

A nutrient-packed smoothie bowl filled with a variety of berries and protein to kickstart your day.

Ingredients:

- 1 cup mixed berries such as strawberries, blueberries, raspberries
- 1 banana
- 1 cup Greek yogurt
- 1 scoop vanilla protein powder
- 1 tablespoon of honey or preferred sweetener of choice

Prep Time: 5 minutes **Freezing Time: 24 hours** **Serving Size: 2**

Instructions:

1. In a blender, combine the mixed berries, banana, Greek yogurt, protein powder, and sweetener. Blend until smooth.
2. Transfer the mixture into the Ninja Creami pint container.
3. Place the lid on the container and freeze for at least 24 hours.
4. After freezing, insert the container into the Ninja Creami machine.
5. Select the 'Smoothie Bowl' program and start the machine.
6. Once the cycle is complete, check the consistency. If it's too thick, use the 'Re-spin' option.
7. Serve in a bowl and enjoy!

Nutrition Information per Serving: Calories: 220 | Total Fat: 2g (Saturated Fat: 1g, Trans Fat: 0g) | Cholesterol: 10mg | Sodium: 60mg | Protein: 16g | Carbohydrate: 38g (Dietary Fiber: 4g) | Phosphorus: 150mg | Potassium: 400mg | Calcium: 150mg

Health Benefits

- Boosts immune system
- Rich in antioxidants
- Supports digestive health

Scientific Benefits

- Berries are high in antioxidants, which can help protect the body from free radical damage.
- Greek yogurt offers probiotics that aid in maintaining gut health and promoting digestion.

Human Experience

" The Berry Protein Power Bowl is my preferred morning meal. It's not just tasty but also sustains my energy levels and keeps me satisfied until lunchtime."

Caution and Precaution

- Hey, watch out for any allergies to berries or dairy before you dig in.
- And make sure those ingredients are all blended up nice and smooth to avoid any choking scares, alright?

Safety Measure

- Pop that smoothie bowl into a trusty airtight container and slide it into the fridge.
- Make sure that container's squeaky clean before you stash it away to fend off any nasty bacteria.

Tropical Muscle Builder

A protein-rich smoothie bowl that transports you to the tropics with its blend of exotic fruits and creamy texture.

Ingredients:

- 1 cup frozen mango chunks
- 1/2 cup frozen pineapple chunks
- 1 banana
- 1 cup coconut milk
- 1 scoop vanilla protein powder

⏱ Prep Time: 5 minutes   ⏱ Freezing Time: 24 hours   🍽 Serving Size: 2

Instructions

1. In a blender, combine the mango, pineapple, banana, coconut milk, and protein powder. Blend until smooth.
2. Transfer the mixture into the Ninja Creami pint container.
3. Place the lid on the container and freeze for at least 24 hours.
4. After freezing, insert the container into the Ninja Creami machine.
5. Select the 'Smoothie Bowl' program and start the machine.
6. Once the cycle is complete, check the consistency. If it's too thick, use the 'Re-spin' option.
7. Serve in a bowl and enjoy!

Nutrition Information per Serving: Calories: 300 | Total Fat: 12g (Saturated Fat: 10g, Trans Fat: 0g) | Cholesterol: 0mg | Sodium: 30mg | Protein: 15g | Carbohydrate: 38g (Dietary Fiber: 4g) | Phosphorus: 120mg | Potassium: 500mg | Calcium: 50mg

Health Benefits

- Supports muscle growth and repair
- Boosts energy levels
- Hydrates and nourishes the body

Scientific Benefits

- Mango and pineapple are rich in vitamins and minerals that support overall health.
- Coconut milk provides healthy fats that can help with energy production.

Human Experience

" After workouts, I indulge in the Tropical Muscle Builder for its refreshing taste and muscle-recovery benefits."

Caution and Precaution

- Hold up, check if anyone around got a thing for tropical fruits like mango or pineapple.

- And when you're wrestling with that blender, just make sure it's locked tight to avoid any tropical messes, got it?

Safety Measure

- Once you've whipped up your tropical treat, pour any leftovers into a snug glass jar. Seal it up nice and tight to keep that goodness fresh.
- And hey, don't forget to label with the date so you know when it's still good.

Green Warrior Bowl

A vibrant and nutrient-packed smoothie bowl that's perfect for a refreshing and energizing start to the day.

Ingredients

- 1 cup spinach leaves
- 1/2 cup frozen avocado chunks
- 1 banana
- 1 cup almond milk
- 1 scoop vanilla protein powder

Prep Time: 15 minutes   **Freezing Time: 24 hours**   **Serving Size: 2**

Instructions:

1. In a blender, combine the spinach, avocado, banana, almond milk, and protein powder. Blend until smooth.
2. Transfer the mixture into the Ninja Creami pint container.
3. Place the lid on the container and freeze for at least 24 hours.
4. After freezing, insert the container into the Ninja Creami machine.
5. Select the 'Smoothie Bowl' program and start the machine.
6. Once the cycle is complete, check the consistency. If it's too thick, use the 'Re-spin' option.
7. Serve in a bowl and enjoy!

Nutrition Information per Serving: Calories: 220 | Total Fat: 9g (Saturated Fat: 1g, Trans Fat: 0g) | Cholesterol: 0mg | Sodium: 90mg | Protein: 12g | Carbohydrate: 28g (Dietary Fiber: 6g) | Phosphorus: 120mg | Potassium: 600mg | Calcium: 150mg

Health Benefits

- Supports immune function and energy levels
- Rich in fiber and healthy fats
- Promotes healthy skin and digestion

Scientific Benefits

- Spinach is high in iron and vitamins A and C, which are essential for immune health.
- Avocado provides monounsaturated fats that are beneficial for heart health.

Human Experience

" The Green Warrior Bowl is my top choice for a fast and nutritious breakfast. It's so easy to make and keeps me full until lunch."

Caution and Precaution

- Those with sensitivities to spinach or nuts should be cautious.
- Check the consistency of the smoothie before freezing to ensure it's not too thick, which could strain the blender motor.

Safety Measure

- Use BPA-free freezer-safe containers to store the frozen smoothie and avoid chemical leaching.
- Leave some space at the top of the container to allow for expansion during freezing, preventing leaks or cracks

Antioxidant Acai Boost

A delicious and antioxidant-rich smoothie bowl that's perfect for a nutritious and refreshing snack or breakfast.

Ingredients:

- 1 acai berry puree packet

- 1/2 cup mixed berries such as strawberries, blueberries, raspberries
- 1 banana
- 1 cup Greek yogurt
- 1 scoop vanilla protein powder

⏲ Prep Time: 15 minutes ⏲ Freezing Time: 24 hours 🍽 Serving Size: 2

1. Instructions:
2. In a blender, combine the acai berry puree, mixed berries, banana, Greek yogurt, and protein powder. Blend until smooth.
3. Transfer the mixture into the Ninja Creami pint container.
4. Place the lid on the container and freeze for at least 24 hours.
5. After freezing, insert the container into the Ninja Creami machine.
6. Select the 'Smoothie Bowl' program and start the machine.
7. Once the cycle is complete, check the consistency. If it's too thick, use the 'Re-spin' option.
8. Serve in a bowl and enjoy!

Nutrition Information per Serving: Calories: 250 | Total Fat: 4g (Saturated Fat: 1g, Trans Fat: 0g) | Cholesterol: 10mg | Sodium: 70mg | Protein: 18g | Carbohydrate: 38g (Dietary Fiber: 5g) | Phosphorus: 160mg | Potassium: 450mg | Calcium: 180mg

Health Benefits

- Boosts energy and immune system
- Rich in antioxidants and probiotics
- Supports digestion and heart health

Scientific Benefits

- Acai berries are recognized for their abundant antioxidants, which combat harmful free radicals in the body.
- Greek yogurt provides valuable probiotics that support digestive wellness.

Human Experience

" I rely on the Antioxidant Acai Boost for a convenient and nutritious morning meal. It's so refreshing and keeps me energized throughout the day."

Caution and Precaution

- Watch for any allergies to acai berries or dairy in the ingredients.
- Ensure the acai berry puree is properly blended with other ingredients to avoid lumps or chunks.

Safety Measure

- Store any extra smoothie in individual portion-sized containers for convenient grab-and-go snacks.
- Seal the containers tightly to prevent freezer burn and maintain the smoothie's flavor and texture.

Pumpkin Spice Recovery Bowl

A seasonal and comforting smoothie bowl infused with the flavors of pumpkin and warm spices, perfect for post-workout recovery.

Ingredients:

- 1 cup pumpkin puree
- 1 banana
- 1 scoop vanilla protein powder
- 1 teaspoon pumpkin pie spice
- 1 cup almond milk

Prep Time: 25 minutes **Freezing Time: 24 hours** **Serving Size: 2**

Instructions:

1. In a blender, combine the pumpkin puree, banana, protein powder, pumpkin pie spice, and almond milk. Blend until smooth.
2. Transfer the mixture into the Ninja Creami pint container.
3. Place the lid on the container and freeze for at least 24 hours.
4. After freezing, insert the container into the Ninja Creami machine.

5. Select the 'Smoothie Bowl' program and start the machine.

6. Once the cycle is complete, check the consistency. If it's too thick, use the 'Re-spin' option.

7. Serve in a bowl and enjoy!

Nutrition Information per Serving: Calories: 180 | Total Fat: 3g (Saturated Fat: 0g, Trans Fat: 0g) | Cholesterol: 0mg | Sodium: 80mg | Protein: 15g | Carbohydrate: 28g (Dietary Fiber: 5g) | Phosphorus: 150mg | Potassium: 400mg | Calcium: 200mg

Health Benefits:

- Supports muscle recovery and immune health
- Rich in vitamins A and C
- Aids in digestion and provides sustained energy

Scientific Benefits

- Pumpkin is high in beta-carotene, which is converted to vitamin A in the body and supports immune function.
- The spices in pumpkin pie spice, like cinnamon and nutmeg, have anti-inflammatory properties.

Human Experience

"The Pumpkin Spice Recovery Bowl is my favorite way to refuel after a workout in the fall. It's so comforting and satisfying."

Caution and Precaution

- Check for any allergies to pumpkin or spices like cinnamon and nutmeg.
- When blending hot liquids, ensure the blender lid is properly vented to release steam and prevent pressure build-up.

Safety Measure

- Allow the smoothie mixture to cool completely before transferring it to the freezer to avoid temperature shock and cracking of the containers

Mango Lassi Lift

A creamy and exotic smoothie bowl inspired by the traditional Indian mango lassi, with added protein for a nourishing boost.

Ingredients:

- 1 cup frozen mango chunks
- 1 cup Greek yogurt
- 1 scoop vanilla protein powder
- 1 tablespoon of honey or preferred sweetener of choice
- 1/2 teaspoon ground cardamom

Prep Time: 20 minutes   Freezing Time: 24 hours   Serving Size: 2

Instructions

1. In a blender, combine the mango chunks, Greek yogurt, protein powder, sweetener, and cardamom. Blend until smooth.
2. Transfer the mixture into the Ninja Creami pint container.
3. Place the lid on the container and freeze for at least 24 hours.
4. After freezing, insert the container into the Ninja Creami machine.
5. Select the 'Smoothie Bowl' program and start the machine.
6. Once the cycle is complete, check the consistency. If it's too thick, use the 'Re-spin' option.
7. Serve in a bowl and enjoy!

Nutrition Information per Serving: Calories: 240 | Total Fat: 3g (Saturated Fat: 1g, Trans Fat: 0g) | Cholesterol: 10mg | Sodium: 80mg | Protein: 20g | Carbohydrate: 36g (Dietary Fiber: 2g) | Phosphorus: 200mg | Potassium: 400mg | Calcium: 250mg

Health Benefits

- Provides a good source of protein and probiotics
- Rich in vitamins A and C for immune support
- Aids in digestion and promotes gut health

Scientific Benefits

- Mangoes are high in antioxidants and vitamin C, which can help boost the immune system.
- Greek yogurt contains probiotics that are beneficial for gut health.

Human Experience

"The Mango Lassi Lift is a refreshing and satisfying treat. It's perfect for a post-workout snack or a light breakfast, and it always leaves me feeling energized."

Caution and Precaution

- Check for any allergies to mango or dairy before consuming.
- Avoid overfilling the blender to prevent spillage or leaks during blending.

Safety Measure

- Store the smoothie bowl in the freezer in an upright position to prevent spillage or deformation of the container.
- Place the container on a stable surface in the freezer to prevent tipping or accidental spills.

Blueberry Maple Muscle

A sweet and nutritious smoothie bowl packed with blueberries and protein, perfect for muscle recovery and a healthy start to the day.

Ingredients:

- 1 cup frozen blueberries
- 1 banana
- 1 scoop vanilla protein powder
- 1 cup almond milk
- 1 tablespoon of maple syrup or preferred sweetener of choice

Prep Time: 25 minutes **Freezing Time: 24 hours** **Serving Size: 2**

Instructions:

1. In a blender, combine the blueberries, banana, protein powder, almond milk, and maple syrup. Blend until smooth.
2. Transfer the mixture into the Ninja Creami pint container.
3. Place the lid on the container and freeze for at least 24 hours.
4. After freezing, insert the container into the Ninja Creami machine.
5. Select the 'Smoothie Bowl' program and start the machine.
6. Once the cycle is complete, check the consistency. If it's too thick, use the 'Re-spin' option.
7. Serve in a bowl and enjoy!

Nutrition Information per Serving: Calories: 220 | Total Fat: 3g (Saturated Fat: 0g, Trans Fat: 0g) | Cholesterol: 0mg | Sodium: 100mg | Protein: 15g | Carbohydrate: 38g (Dietary Fiber: 5g) | Phosphorus: 150mg | Potassium: 400mg | Calcium: 200mg

Health Benefits

- Supports muscle recovery and growth
- Rich in antioxidants for overall health
- Provides a natural energy boost

Scientific Benefits

- Blueberries are known for their high antioxidant content, which can help reduce inflammation and protect against oxidative stress.
- Ensuring an ample protein intake is crucial for the repair and growth of muscles, which is why this bowl is perfect for aiding in post-workout recovery.

Human Experience

"The Blueberry Maple Muscle bowl is my favorite way to refuel after a morning workout. It's delicious, satisfying, and gives me the energy I need for the rest of the day."

Caution and Precaution

- Individuals with allergies to blueberries or maple syrup should avoid this recipe.

Safety Measure

- Divide the smoothie into smaller portions and store them in silicone freezer bags to save space and reduce plastic waste.
- Remove any excess air from the freezer bags before sealing to prevent freezer burn and maintain freshness.

Sunrise Citrus Surge

A refreshing and invigorating smoothie bowl that combines the bright flavors of citrus fruits with a protein boost for a perfect morning pick-me-up.

Ingredients:

- 1/2 cup orange juice
- 1/2 cup frozen peaches
- 1 banana
- 1 scoop vanilla protein powder
- 1/2 teaspoon turmeric powder

Prep Time: 20 minutes **Freezing Time: 24 hours** **Serving Size: 2**

Instructions:

1. In a blender, combine the orange juice, peaches, banana, protein powder, and turmeric powder. Blend until smooth.
2. Transfer the mixture into the Ninja Creami pint container.
3. Place the lid on the container and freeze for at least 24 hours.
4. After freezing, insert the container into the Ninja Creami machine.
5. Select the 'Smoothie Bowl' program and start the machine.
6. Once the cycle is complete, check the consistency. If it's too thick, use the 'Re-spin' option.
7. Serve in a bowl and enjoy!

Nutrition Information per Serving: Calories: 180 | Total Fat: 1g (Saturated Fat: 0g, Trans Fat: 0g) | Cholesterol: 0mg | Sodium: 50mg | Protein: 15g | Carbohydrate: 32g (Dietary Fiber: 3g) | Phosphorus: 100mg | Potassium: 500mg | Calcium: 150mg

Health Benefits

- Boosts energy and immunity
- Rich in vitamin C and antioxidants
- Aids in inflammation reduction and digestion

Scientific Benefits

- Orange juice and peaches are high in vitamin C, which is essential for immune function and skin health.
- Turmeric contains curcumin, which has anti-inflammatory and antioxidant properties.

Human Experience

"I love starting my day with the Sunrise Citrus Surge bowl. It's so refreshing and gives me a great energy boost in the morning."

Caution and Precaution

- Watch for any citrus allergies, especially to ingredients like oranges or lemons.
- Ensure the blender lid is securely in place to prevent splattering when blending citrus fruits.

Safety Measure

- Transfer the smoothie mixture into silicone ice cube trays to create individual frozen cubes for easy portioning and blending.
- Label the ice cube trays with the date of preparation to keep track of freshness and prevent freezer burn

Nut-Based Recipe

Peanut Butter Cup Pro Bowl

A creamy and indulgent smoothie bowl that combines the rich flavors of peanut butter and chocolate for a satisfying treat.

Ingredients:

- 1 banana
- 1/4 cup natural peanut butter

- 1 scoop chocolate protein powder
- 1 cup almond milk

⏲ Prep Time: 10 minutes   ⏲ Freezing Time: 24 hours   ⏱ Serving Size: 2

Instructions:

1. In a blender, combine the banana, peanut butter, chocolate protein powder, and almond milk. Blend until smooth.
2. Transfer the mixture into the Ninja Creami pint container.
3. Place the lid on the container and freeze for at least 24 hours.
4. After freezing, insert the container into the Ninja Creami machine.
5. Select the 'Smoothie Bowl' program and start the machine.
6. Once the cycle is complete, check the consistency. If it's too thick, use the 'Re-spin' option.
7. Serve in a bowl and enjoy!

Nutrition Information per Serving: Calories: 330 | Total Fat: 18g (Saturated Fat: 3g, Trans Fat: 0g) | Cholesterol: 0mg | Sodium: 200mg | Protein: 20g | Carbohydrate: 28g (Dietary Fiber: 4g) | Phosphorus: 180mg | Potassium: 500mg | Calcium: 150mg

Health Benefits
- Provides a high-protein, satisfying snack. Rich in healthy fats for sustained energy
- Supports muscle recovery and growth

Scientific Benefits
- Peanut butter is a good source of monounsaturated fats, which are beneficial for heart health.
- Chocolate protein powder provides essential amino acids for muscle repair.

Human Experience
"I'm obsessed with the Peanut Butter Cup Pro Bowl. It's like having dessert for breakfast, but it's actually good for me!"

Caution and Precaution
- Individuals with peanut allergies should avoid this recipe.

- Double-check the blender lid to prevent any leaks or spills, especially when blending thick ingredients like peanut butter.

Safety Measure

- Store the smoothie bowl in a shallow container to facilitate quicker thawing when ready to eat.
- Keep the container away from strong-smelling foods in the freezer to prevent flavor contamination.

Chocolate-Based Recipe

Cafe Mocha Energizer

A coffee-infused smoothie bowl that combines the rich flavors of chocolate and espresso for an energizing start to your day.

Ingredients:

- 1 banana
- 1 scoop chocolate protein powder
- 1/2 cup brewed espresso, cooled
- 1 tablespoon cocoa powder
- 1 cup almond milk

Prep Time: 10 minutes **Freezing Time: 24 hours** **Serving Size: 2**

Instructions:

1. In a blender, combine the banana, chocolate protein powder, espresso, cocoa powder, and almond milk. Blend until smooth.
2. Transfer the mixture into the Ninja Creami pint container. Place the lid on the container and freeze for at least 24 hours.
3. After freezing, insert the container into the Ninja Creami machine.
4. Select the 'Smoothie Bowl' program and start the machine.
5. Once the cycle is complete, check the consistency. If it's too thick, use the 'Re-spin' option.
6. Serve in a bowl and enjoy!

Nutrition Information per Serving: Calories: 200 | Total Fat: 4g (Saturated Fat: 1g, Trans Fat: 0g) | Cholesterol: 10mg | Sodium: 100mg | Protein: 15g | Carbohydrate: 28g (Dietary Fiber: 3g) | Phosphorus: 180mg | Potassium: 400mg | Calcium: 200mg

Health Benefits

- Boosts energy and mental alertness. Provides a good source of protein and antioxidants
- Supports muscle recovery

Scientific Benefits

- Espresso contains caffeine, which can improve focus and increase energy levels.
- Cocoa powder is rich in flavonoids, which have been linked to heart health and improved circulation.

Human Experience

"The Cafe Mocha Energizer is my go-to breakfast when I need an extra boost. It's like having my morning coffee and breakfast all in one delicious bowl."

Caution and Precaution

- Ensure the espresso is cooled before blending to prevent damage to the blender's plastic components.

Safety Measure

- Store the prepared smoothie bowl in a thermally insulated container to keep it chilled during transportation.
- Avoid storing the smoothie bowl near strong-smelling foods in the refrigerator to maintain its flavor profile.

Fruit-Based Sorbet Recipes

Mango Protein Sorbet

A tropical and refreshing sorbet made with sweet mangoes and a boost of protein for a guilt-free treat.

Ingredients:

- 2 cups frozen mango chunks
- 1 scoop vanilla protein powder
- 1/2 cup coconut water or water
- 1 tablespoon of honey or preferred sweetener of choice

⏰**Prep Time: 5 minutes** ⏰ **Freezing Time: 24 hours** 🍽 **Serving Size: 2**

Instructions:

1. In a blender, combine the frozen mango chunks, protein powder, coconut water, and sweetener. Blend until smooth.
2. Transfer the mixture into the Ninja Creami pint container.
3. Place the lid on the container and freeze for at least 24 hours.
4. After freezing, insert the container into the Ninja Creami machine.
5. Select the 'Sorbet' program and start the machine.
6. Once the cycle is complete, serve the Mango Protein Sorbet and enjoy!

Nutrition Information per Serving: Calories: 150 | Total Fat: 1g (Saturated Fat: 0g, Trans Fat: 0g) | Cholesterol: 0mg | Sodium: 50mg | Protein: 10g | Carbohydrate: 28g

Health Benefits

- It offers a good amount of protein and vitamin C
- Hydrates and refreshes the body

Scientific Benefits

- Mangoes are rich in antioxidants, particularly beta-carotene, which has been shown to support eye health and boost the immune system.

Human Experience

" I find this Mango Protein Sorbet to be a fantastic option after my workout. It's so refreshing and helps me refuel without feeling heavy."

Cautions and Precautions

- Check the protein powder ingredients for allergens like soy or dairy if you have dietary restrictions.
- Exercise caution when blending frozen mango chunks to avoid damaging the blender blades.

Safety Measures

- Store the sorbet in an air-tight container to prevent freezer burn and maintain freshness.
- Store the sorbet away from strong-smelling foods in the freezer to prevent flavor contamination.

Strawberry Banana Protein Sorbet

A classic combination of strawberries and bananas blended into a smooth sorbet with added protein for a satisfying treat.

Ingredients:

- 1 cup frozen strawberries
- 1 frozen banana
- 1 scoop vanilla protein powder
- 1/2 cup almond milk
- 1 tablespoon of honey or preferred sweetener of choice

Prep Time: 10 minutes Freezing Time: 24 hours Serving Size: 2

Instructions:

1. In a blender, combine the frozen strawberries, banana, protein powder, almond milk, and sweetener. Blend until smooth.

2. Transfer the mixture into the Ninja Creami pint container.

3. Place the lid on the container and freeze for at least 24 hours.

4. After freezing, insert the container into the Ninja Creami machine.

5. Select the 'Sorbet' program and start the machine.

6. Once the cycle is complete, serve the Strawberry Banana Protein Sorbet and enjoy!

Nutrition Information per Serving: Calories: 160 | Total Fat: 1g (Saturated Fat: 0g, Trans Fat: 0g) | Cholesterol: 0mg | Sodium: 60mg | Protein: 10g | Carbohydrate: 32g (Dietary Fiber: 3g) | Phosphorus: 110mg | Potassium: 400mg | Calcium: 120mg

Health Benefits

- Provides a good source of protein and fiber
- Rich in vitamins and minerals, including vitamin C and potassium

Scientific Benefits

- Strawberries and bananas are both high in antioxidants, which can help reduce inflammation and protect against chronic diseases.

Human Experience

"The Strawberry Banana Protein Sorbet is my favorite way to satisfy my sweet tooth. It's so creamy and delicious, and I love that it's packed with nutrients."

Cautions and Precautions

Exercise caution when blending frozen fruits to prevent damage to the blender motor.

Ensure the sorbet mixture is smooth before freezing to avoid uneven texture.

Safety Measures

- Store sorbet in layers with parchment paper between to prevent sticking.
- Keep the sorbet container away from the freezer door to prevent temperature fluctuations.

Blueberry Protein Sorbet

A delicious and antioxidant-rich sorbet made with blueberries and protein powder for a healthy and refreshing treat.

Ingredients:

- 2 cups frozen blueberries
- 1 scoop vanilla protein powder
- 1/2 cup coconut water or water
- 1 tablespoon of honey or preferred sweetener of choice

Prep Time: 15 minutes **Freezing Time: 24 hours** **Serving Size: 2**

Instructions:

1. In a blender, combine the frozen blueberries, protein powder, coconut water, and sweetener. Blend until smooth.
2. Transfer the mixture into the Ninja Creami pint container.
3. Place the lid on the container and freeze for at least 24 hours.
4. After freezing, insert the container into the Ninja Creami machine.
5. Select the 'Sorbet' program and start the machine.
6. Once the cycle is complete, serve the Blueberry Protein Sorbet and enjoy!

Nutrition Information per Serving: Calories: 140 | Total Fat: 1g (Saturated Fat: 0g, Trans Fat: 0g) | Cholesterol: 0mg | Sodium: 50mg | Protein: 10g | Carbohydrate: 26g (Dietary Fiber: 4g) | Phosphorus: 100mg | Potassium: 200mg | Calcium: 100mg

Health Benefits
- Provides a good source of protein and antioxidants
- Supports brain health and heart health

Scientific Benefits
- Blueberries are known for their high levels of antioxidants, particularly flavonoids, which have been linked to improved cognitive function and reduced risk of heart disease.

Human Experience
" he Blueberry Protein Sorbet is equally delightful, offering a refreshing and fulfilling treat. I love that it's packed with antioxidants and protein, making it a perfect guilt-free treat."

Cautions and Precautions

- Do not overload the blender with frozen blueberries to prevent strain on the motor.
- Ensure even distribution of protein powder to avoid clumps in the sorbet mixture.
- Use fresh or properly frozen blueberries to achieve the best flavor and texture.

Safety Measures

- Use a container size suitable for the amount of sorbet to minimize excess air space.
- Consume the sorbet within a reasonable timeframe to maintain optimal freshness and flavor.

Pineapple Coconut Protein Sorbet

A tropical and refreshing sorbet that combines the sweet flavors of pineapple and coconut with a boost of protein for a satisfying and healthy dessert.

Ingredients:

- 2 cups frozen pineapple chunks
- 1 scoop vanilla protein powder
- 1/2 cup coconut milk
- 1 tablespoon of honey or preferred sweetener of choice

Prep Time: 10 minutes Freezing Time: 24 hours Serving Size: 2

Instructions:

1. In a blender, combine the frozen pineapple chunks, protein powder, coconut milk, and sweetener. Blend until smooth.
2. Transfer the mixture into the Ninja Creami pint container.
3. Place the lid on the container and freeze for at least 24 hours.
4. After freezing, insert the container into the Ninja Creami machine.
5. Select the 'Sorbet' program and start the machine.
6. Once the cycle is complete, serve the Pineapple Coconut Protein Sorbet and enjoy!

Nutrition Information per Serving: Calories: 180 | Total Fat: 6g (Saturated Fat: 5g, Trans Fat: 0g) | Cholesterol: 0mg | Sodium: 45mg | Protein: 10g | Carbohydrate: 26g (Dietary Fiber: 2g) | Phosphorus: 100mg | Potassium: 250mg | Calcium: 100mg

Health Benefits

- Provides a good source of protein and healthy fats

- Abundant in essential nutrients like vitamin C and manganese.

Scientific Benefits

- Pineapple contains bromelain, an enzyme that has been shown to have anti-inflammatory properties and may aid in digestion.

- Coconut milk is a good source of medium-chain triglycerides (MCTs), which can provide a quick source of energy.

Human Experience

"The Pineapple Coconut Protein Sorbet is like a mini vacation in a bowl. It's so creamy and flavorful, and I love that it's a healthier alternative to traditional ice cream."

Cautions and Precautions

- Shake the coconut milk can before use to ensure uniform consistency.
- Avoid using warm coconut milk to prevent premature melting of the sorbet mixture.

Safety Measures

- Seal the sorbet container tightly to prevent moisture loss and crystallization.
- Keep the sorbet container clean to prevent contamination and preserve flavor integrity.

Nut-Based Sorbet Recipes

Almond Chocolate Protein Sorbet

A rich and nutty sorbet that combines the flavors of almonds and chocolate with a boost of protein.

Ingredients:

- 2 cups almond milk

- 1 scoop chocolate protein powder
- 1/2 cup cocoa powder
- 1/2 cup granulated sugar
- 1/2 cup almond butter

⏲ **Prep Time: 15 minutes** ⏲ **Freezing Time: 24 hours** 🍽 **Serving Size: 4**

Instructions:

1. In a blender, combine the almond milk, chocolate protein powder, cocoa powder, sugar, and almond butter. Blend until smooth.
2. Transfer the mixture into the Ninja Creami pint container.
3. Place the lid on the container and freeze for at least 24 hours.
4. After freezing, insert the container into the Ninja Creami machine.
5. Select the 'Sorbet' program and start the machine.
6. Once the cycle is complete, check the consistency. If it's too thick, use the 'Re-spin' option.
7. Serve in bowls and enjoy the Almond Chocolate Protein Sorbet!

Nutrition Information per Serving: Calories: 300 | Total Fat: 16g (Saturated Fat: 2g, Trans Fat: 0g) | Cholesterol: 0mg | Sodium: 100mg | Protein: 10g | Carbohydrate: 34g (Dietary Fiber: 6g) | Phosphorus: 200mg | Potassium: 300mg | Calcium: 150mg

Health Benefits
- Provides a good source of protein and healthy fats
- Almond butter is rich in vitamin E and magnesium

Scientific Benefits
- Almonds contain monounsaturated fats that can help lower bad cholesterol levels and reduce the risk of heart disease.
- Cocoa powder is high in flavonoids, which have been shown to improve blood flow and lower blood pressure.

Human Experience

"The Almond Chocolate Protein Sorbet is my go-to when I'm craving something sweet but still want to stick to my fitness goals. It's so creamy and satisfying!"

Cautions and Precautions

- Ensure the almond butter is properly blended to avoid chunks that may clog the blender.
- Stir granulated sugar thoroughly into the mixture to ensure it dissolves completely.
- Check the sorbet consistency before freezing to ensure its smooth and uniform.

Safety Measures

- Ensure the container is tightly sealed guards against air exposure, thus preserving its freshness.
- Place the sorbet container away from the freezer door to maintain a consistent temperature.

Peanut Butter Protein Sorbet

A creamy and indulgent sorbet that blends the rich flavor of peanut butter with a protein boost for a satisfying treat.

Ingredients:

- 2 cups almond milk
- 1 scoop vanilla protein powder
- 1/2 cup natural peanut butter
- 1/2 cup granulated sugar

Prep Time: 10 minutes **Freezing Time: 24 hours** **Serving Size: 4**

Instructions:

1. In a blender, combine the almond milk, vanilla protein powder, peanut butter, and sugar. Blend until smooth.
2. Transfer the mixture into the Ninja Creami pint container.
3. Place the lid on the container and freeze for at least 24 hours.
4. After freezing, insert the container into the Ninja Creami machine.
5. Select the 'Sorbet' program and start the machine.

6. Once the cycle is complete, check the consistency. If it's too thick, use the 'Re-spin' option.

7. Serve in bowls and enjoy the Peanut Butter Protein Sorbet!

Nutrition Information per Serving: Calories: 320 | Total Fat: 18g (Saturated Fat: 3g, Trans Fat: 0g) | Cholesterol: 0mg | Sodium: 150mg | Protein: 12g | Carbohydrate: 30g (Dietary Fiber: 2g) | Phosphorus: 220mg | Potassium: 350mg | Calcium: 200mg

Health Benefits

- Provides a good source of protein and healthy fats

- peanut butter is renowned for its high content of heart-healthy monounsaturated fats.

Scientific Benefits

- Peanuts are a good source of antioxidants, which can help protect cells from damage.

- Protein is essential for muscle repair and growth, making this sorbet a great post-workout snack.

Human Experience

"The Peanut Butter Protein Sorbet is like a dream come true for peanut butter lovers. It's so rich and creamy, and I love that it's packed with protein."

Cautions and Precautions

- Blend peanut butter thoroughly to avoid clumps and ensure a smooth texture.
- Ensure thorough mixing of all ingredients to achieve a uniform flavor profile.

Safety Measures

- Use a container with minimal air space to prevent ice crystal formation and maintain texture.
- Consume the sorbet within a reasonable timeframe to enjoy optimal flavor and texture.

Cashew Vanilla Protein Sorbet

A smooth and creamy sorbet that combines the subtle nuttiness of cashews with the sweetness of vanilla and a protein boost.

Ingredients:

- 2 cups cashew milk

- 1 scoop vanilla protein powder
- 1/2 cup cashew butter
- 1/2 cup granulated sugar
- 1 teaspoon vanilla extract

⏰Prep Time: 15 minutes ⏲ Freezing Time: 24 hours 🍽 Serving Size: 4

Instructions:

1. In a blender, combine the cashew milk, vanilla protein powder, cashew butter, sugar, and vanilla extract. Blend until smooth.
2. Transfer the mixture into the Ninja Creami pint container.
3. Place the lid on the container and freeze for at least 24 hours.
4. After freezing, insert the container into the Ninja Creami machine.
5. Select the 'Sorbet' program and start the machine.
6. Once the cycle is complete, check the consistency. If it's too thick, use the 'Re-spin' option.
7. Serve in bowls and enjoy the Cashew Vanilla Protein Sorbet!

Nutrition Information per Serving: Calories: 320 | Total Fat: 18g (Saturated Fat: 3g, Trans Fat: 0g) | Cholesterol: 0mg | Sodium: 100mg | Protein: 12g | Carbohydrate: 32g (Dietary Fiber: 1g) | Phosphorus: 220mg | Potassium: 300mg | Calcium: 200mg

Health Benefits
- Provides a good source of protein and healthy fats
- Cashew butter is rich in essential vitamins and minerals

Scientific Benefits
- Cashews contain heart-healthy fats and are a good source of antioxidants.
- Vanilla has been shown to have anti-inflammatory properties and can help reduce anxiety.

Human Experience
"The Cashew Vanilla Protein Sorbet is so smooth and delicious. It's a great way to satisfy my sweet tooth while getting some extra protein."

Cautions and Precautions

- Use the appropriate amount of vanilla extract to avoid overpowering the delicate cashew flavor.
- Use smooth cashew butter to ensure a creamy texture in the sorbet.

Safety Measures

- Ensure the container is tightly sealed guards against air exposure, thus preserving its freshness..
- Ensure the sorbet container is placed flat in the freezer to achieve uniform freezing and texture.

Unique Flavor Combinations

Matcha Green Tea Protein Sorbet

A refreshing and antioxidant-rich sorbet that combines the earthy flavors of matcha green tea with a protein boost.

Ingredients:

- 2 cups water
- 3/4 cup granulated sugar
- 1 scoop vanilla protein powder
- 2 tablespoons matcha green tea powder
- 1 tablespoon lemon juice

⏲ **Prep Time: 15 minutes** ⏲ **Freezing Time: 24 hours** 🍽 **Serving Size: 4**

Instructions:

1. In a saucepan, combine the water and sugar. Heat over medium heat, stirring continuously until the sugar has completely dissolved.
2. Remove from heat and let cool. Once cooled, whisk in the protein powder, matcha green tea powder, and lemon juice until smooth.
3. Transfer the mixture into the Ninja Creami pint container.
4. Place the lid on the container and freeze for at least 24 hours.
5. After freezing, insert the container into the Ninja Creami machine.
6. Select the 'Sorbet' program and start the machine.

7. Once the cycle is complete, serve the Matcha Green Tea Protein Sorbet in bowls and enjoy!

Nutrition Information per Serving: Calories: 180 | Total Fat: 0g (Saturated Fat: 0g, Trans Fat: 0g) | Cholesterol: 0mg | Sodium: 40mg | Protein: 8g | Carbohydrate: 36g (Dietary Fiber: 1g) | Phosphorus: 100mg | Potassium: 120mg | Calcium: 80mg

Health Benefits

- Provides a good source of antioxidants and protein.
- Matcha green tea is known for its potential to boost metabolism and improve concentration.

Scientific Benefits

- Matcha contains a high level of catechins, a type of antioxidant that has been linked to reduced inflammation and improved heart health.

Human Experience

"I never knew a sorbet could be so satisfying! The Matcha Green Tea Protein Sorbet is the perfect treat after a workout or on a hot day."

Cautions and Precautions

- Whisk matcha green tea powder thoroughly into the mixture to prevent clumps.
- Ensure granulated sugar is fully dissolved in the mixture to avoid grainy texture.
- Use the recommended amount of lemon juice to balance the flavors without overpowering the matcha.

Safety Measures

- Keep the sorbet container in the coldest part of the freezer to prevent thawing and refreezing.
- Label the container with the date of preparation for easy tracking of freshness.

Lavender Honey Protein Sorbet

A delicate and floral sorbet that combines the soothing aroma of lavender with the natural sweetness of honey, enhanced with a touch of protein.

Ingredients:

- 2 cups water
- 3/4 cup honey
- 1 scoop vanilla protein powder
- 1 tablespoon dried lavender flowers
- 1 tablespoon lemon juice

Prep Time: 15 minutes **Freezing Time: 24 hours** **Serving Size: 4**

Instructions:

- In a saucepan, combine the water, honey, and lavender flowers. Heat over medium heat, stirring until the honey is dissolved. Simmer for 5 minutes, then remove from heat and let steep for 10 minutes.
- Strain the mixture to remove the lavender flowers, then let cool. Once cooled, whisk in the protein powder and lemon juice until smooth.
- Transfer the mixture into the Ninja Creami pint container.
- Place the lid on the container and freeze for at least 24 hours.
- After freezing, insert the container into the Ninja Creami machine.
- Select the 'Sorbet' program and start the machine.
- Once the cycle is complete, serve the Lavender Honey Protein Sorbet in bowls and enjoy!

Nutrition Information per Serving: Calories: 190 | Total Fat: 0g (Saturated Fat: 0g, Trans Fat: 0g) | Cholesterol: 0mg | Sodium: 40mg | Protein: 8g | Carbohydrate: 42g (Dietary Fiber: 0g) | Phosphorus: 100mg | Potassium: 120mg | Calcium: 80mg

Health Benefits

- Provides a good source of protein and antioxidants

- Lavender is known for its calming properties and may help promote relaxation

Scientific Benefits

- Honey contains antioxidants and has been shown to have antibacterial properties.

Human Experience

"The Lavender Honey Protein Sorbet is like a spa day in a bowl. It's so calming and refreshing, and I love the hint of floral flavor."

Cautions and Precautions

- Ensure proper steeping time for the lavender flowers to avoid overpowering the sorbet with a bitter taste.
- Whisk honey thoroughly into the mixture to prevent clumps and achieve a smooth texture.
- Strain the lavender-infused mixture carefully to remove all solid particles and ensure a smooth texture.
- Adjust the amount of lemon juice to maintain a delicate balance of flavors without making the sorbet too tangy.
- Be cautious of pollen allergies when serving or sharing the sorbet with others.

Safety Measures

- Store the sorbet container away from strong-smelling foods to prevent flavor contamination.
- Consume the sorbet within a reasonable timeframe to enjoy its freshness and fragrance.
- seal the container tightly to prevent air exposure and maintain the aroma of lavender.

Coconut Lime Protein Sorbet

A tropical and zesty sorbet that combines the creamy flavor of coconut with the tangy taste of lime, enhanced with a boost of protein.

Ingredients:

- 2 cups coconut water
- 3/4 cup granulated sugar
- 1 scoop vanilla protein powder

- 1/2 cup coconut milk
- 1/4 cup lime juice
- 1 tablespoon lime zest

⏱ Prep Time: 10 minutes ⏱ Freezing Time: 24 hours 🍽 Serving Size: 4

Instructions:

- In a saucepan, combine the coconut water and sugar. Heat over medium heat, stirring continuously until the sugar is dissolved.
- Remove from heat and let cool. Once cooled, whisk in the protein powder, coconut milk, lime juice, and lime zest until smooth.
- Transfer the mixture into the Ninja Creami pint container.
- Place the lid on the container and freeze for at least 24 hours.
- After freezing, insert the container into the Ninja Creami machine.
- Select the 'Sorbet' program and start the machine.
- Once the cycle is complete, serve the Coconut Lime Protein Sorbet in bowls and enjoy!

Nutrition Information per Serving: Calories: 200 | Total Fat: 3g (Saturated Fat: 3g, Trans Fat: 0g) | Cholesterol: 0mg | Sodium: 60mg | Protein: 8g | Carbohydrate: 36g (Dietary Fiber: 1g) | Phosphorus: 100mg | Potassium: 300mg | Calcium: 80mg

Health Benefits

- Provides a good source of protein and electrolytes
- Coconut water is hydrating and contains minerals such as potassium and magnesium

Scientific Benefits

- Coconut milk contains medium-chain triglycerides which have been linked to improved energy expenditure and weight management.

Human Experience

"The Coconut Lime Protein Sorbet is like a tropical getaway in a bowl. It's so refreshing and light, perfect for a hot day."

Cautions and Precautions

- Use full-fat coconut milk for a creamy texture and avoid light versions, which may result in a watery sorbet.

- Grate lime zest carefully to avoid including the bitter white pith, which can affect the sorbet's flavor.

- Stir granulated sugar thoroughly into the mixture to ensure it dissolves completely and prevents graininess.

- Adjust the amount of lime juice to balance the sweetness of the sorbet without making it too tart.

- Be cautious of citrus allergies when serving or sharing the sorbet with others.

Safety Measures

- Seal the container tightly to prevent air exposure and maintain the freshness of the sorbet.

- Store the sorbet away from strong-smelling foods in the freezer to prevent flavor absorption.

- Thaw the sorbet in the refrigerator to preserve its creamy texture and prevent melting.

- Consume the sorbet within a reasonable timeframe to enjoy its vibrant flavor and texture.

GELATO WITH ADDED PROTEIN

Fruit Based

Tropical Paradise Gelato

A smooth and creamy gelato that transports your taste buds to a tropical paradise with a blend of exotic fruits.

Ingredients:

- 2 cups whole milk
- 1 cup heavy cream
- 3/4 cup granulated sugar
- 1 scoop vanilla protein powder
- 1 cup frozen pineapple chunks
- 1/2 cup frozen mango chunks
- 1/2 cup coconut milk

Prep Time: 10 minutes **Freezing Time: 24 hours** **Serving Size: 4**

Instructions:

1. In a blender, combine the whole milk, heavy cream, sugar, protein powder, pineapple, mango, and coconut milk. Blend until smooth.
2. Transfer the mixture into the Ninja Creami pint container.
3. Place the lid on the container and freeze for at least 24 hours.
4. After freezing, insert the container into the Ninja Creami machine.
5. Select the 'Gelato' program and start the machine.
6. Once the cycle is complete, check the consistency. If it's too thick, use the 'Re-spin' option.
7. Serve in bowls and enjoy the Tropical Paradise Gelato!

Nutrition Information per Serving: Calories: 300 | Total Fat: 16g (Saturated Fat: 11g, Trans Fat: 0g) | Cholesterol: 60mg | Sodium: 50mg | Protein: 7g | Carbohydrate: 34g (Dietary Fiber: 1g) | Phosphorus: 100mg | Potassium: 250mg | Calcium: 150mg

Health Benefits

- It offers a good amount of protein and healthy fats
- Rich in vitamins and minerals from tropical fruits

Scientific Benefits

- Coconut milk is rich in medium-chain triglycerides (MCTs), which the body efficiently absorbs and utilizes as a source of energy.
- Pineapple and mango are rich in vitamins C and A, which are important for immune function and skin health.

Human Experience

"The Tropical Paradise Gelato is like a vacation in a bowl. It's so creamy and full of flavor, and I love the tropical fruit combination."

Cautions and Precautions

- Ensure all fruits are thoroughly washed to remove any dirt or pesticides before using them in the recipe.
- Be cautious while handling the blender blades to avoid any accidental cuts or injuries.
- Store the gelato away from direct sunlight to prevent melting and preserve its freshness.

Safety Measures

- Transfer the gelato into an airtight container to prevent freezer burn and maintain its flavor.
- Place the container in the coldest part of the freezer to ensure proper freezing without any fluctuations in temperature.
- Avoid frequent opening of the freezer door to maintain a consistent temperature and prevent thawing of the gelato.

Peach Melba Magic

A delightful gelato that combines the sweet and juicy flavors of peaches with the tangy taste of raspberries for a classic Peach Melba experience.

Ingredients:

- 2 cups whole milk
- 1 cup heavy cream
- 3/4 cup granulated sugar
- 1 scoop vanilla protein powder
- 1 cup fresh or frozen peaches, diced
- 1/2 cup raspberry puree

Prep Time: 15 minutes   Freezing Time: 24 hours   Serving Size: 4

Instructions:

1. In a blender, combine the whole milk, heavy cream, sugar, and protein powder. Blend until smooth.
2. Transfer the mixture into the Ninja Creami pint container.
3. Place the lid on the container and freeze for at least 24 hours.
4. After freezing, insert the container into the Ninja Creami machine.
5. Select the 'Gelato' program and start the machine.
6. Once the cycle is complete, check the consistency. If it's too thick, use the 'Re-spin' option.
7. Serve in bowls and enjoy the Peach Melba Magic!

Nutrition Information per Serving: Calories: 320 | Total Fat: 18g (Saturated Fat: 11g, Trans Fat: 0g) | Cholesterol: 70mg | Sodium: 60mg | Protein: 7g | Carbohydrate: 36g (Dietary Fiber: 1g) | Phosphorus: 110mg | Potassium: 270mg | Calcium: 160mg

Health Benefits

- Provides a good source of protein and vitamins
- Peaches and raspberries are rich in antioxidants and fiber

Scientific Benefits

- Peaches contain bioactive compounds that have been linked to improved heart health and reduced inflammation.
- Raspberries are high in ellagic acid, a compound with potential anti-cancer properties.

Human Experience

"Peach Melba Magic is my favorite summertime treat. It's so refreshing and has the perfect balance of sweetness and tartness."

Cautions and Precautions

- Use ripe but firm peaches to ensure optimal sweetness and flavor in the gelato.
- Be cautious while handling hot syrup to avoid burns or scalds during the preparation process.
- Keep children away from the kitchen when working with hot ingredients to prevent any accidents or injuries.

Safety Measures

- Store the gelato in shallow containers to allow for quicker freezing and easier scooping.
- Place a layer of plastic wrap directly on the surface of the gelato before sealing the container to prevent ice crystals from forming.
- Avoid storing the gelato near strong-smelling foods to prevent absorption of unwanted odors.

Watermelon Mint Marvel

A refreshing and light gelato that combines the sweet taste of watermelon with a hint of mint for a cooling summer treat.

Ingredients:

- 2 cups watermelon, cubed and seeds removed
- 1 cup whole milk
- 1/2 cup heavy cream
- 3/4 cup granulated sugar
- 1 scoop vanilla protein powder
- 1/4 cup fresh mint leaves, chopped

⏲ Prep Time: 15 minutes ⏲ Freezing Time: 24 hours 🍽 Serving Size: 2

Instructions:

1. In a blender, combine the watermelon, whole milk, heavy cream, sugar, protein powder, and mint leaves. Blend until smooth.
2. Transfer the mixture into the Ninja Creami pint container.
3. Place the lid on the container and freeze for at least 24 hours.
4. After freezing, insert the container into the Ninja Creami machine.
5. Select the 'Gelato' program and start the machine.
6. Once the cycle is complete, check the consistency. If it's too thick, use the 'Re-spin' option.
7. Serve in bowls and enjoy the Watermelon Mint Marvel!

Nutrition Information per Serving: Calories: 280 | Total Fat: 12g (Saturated Fat: 7g, Trans Fat: 0g) | Cholesterol: 45mg | Sodium: 40mg | Protein: 6g | Carbohydrate: 38g (Dietary Fiber: 1g) | Phosphorus: 90mg | Potassium: 200mg | Calcium: 140mg

Health Benefits

- It offers hydration benefits and serves as a valuable source of essential vitamins.
- Watermelon is rich in antioxidants and can help reduce muscle soreness

Scientific Benefits

- Watermelon, on the other hand, boasts lycopene, an antioxidant renowned for its positive impact on heart health and potential in preventing cancer.
- Mint has been shown to have anti-inflammatory properties and can aid in digestion.

Human Experience

" A delightful option for beating the heat, Watermelon Mint Marvel proves to be an ideal refreshment for those scorching summer days. It's so light and refreshing, and the mint adds a wonderful cooling effect.

Cautions and Precautions

- Use seedless watermelon to avoid the hassle of removing seeds before blending.

- Be cautious when adding fresh mint leaves to the blender to avoid over-processing and releasing bitter flavors.
- Check the sweetness of the watermelon before adding additional sweeteners to the gelato mixture.
- Avoid using wilted or discolored mint leaves as they may affect the flavor and appearance of the gelato.
- Keep the blender lid securely in place while blending to prevent any spills or splatters.

Safety Measures

- Transfer the gelato into silicone ice cube trays for individual servings, making it easier to portion and serve.
- Place the ice cube trays on a flat surface in the freezer to ensure even freezing and prevent tipping or spilling.
- Cover the ice cube trays with plastic wrap before placing them in the freezer to prevent freezer burn and contamination.
- Store the gelato cubes in a resealable freezer bag to keep them fresh and protected from freezer odors.

Chocolate Based Gelato

Double Chocolate Chunk Gelato

A rich and indulgent gelato that doubles down on the chocolate for a truly decadent experience.

Ingredients:

- 2 cups whole milk
- 1 cup heavy cream
- 3/4 cup granulated sugar
- 1/2 cup unsweetened cocoa powder
- 1 scoop chocolate protein powder
- 1/2 cup dark chocolate chunks

Prep Time: 10 minutes **Freezing Time: 24 hours** **Serving Size: 2**

Instructions:

1. In a blender, combine the milk, cream, sugar, cocoa powder, and protein powder. Blend until smooth.
2. Transfer the mixture into the Ninja Creami pint container.
3. Place the lid on the container and freeze for at least 24 hours.
4. After freezing, insert the container into the Ninja Creami machine.
5. Select the 'Gelato' program and start the machine.
6. Once the cycle is complete, check the consistency. If it's too thick, use the 'Re-spin' option.
7. Serve in bowls and enjoy the Double Chocolate Chunk Gelato!

Nutrition Information per Serving: Calories: 350 | Total Fat: 22g (Saturated Fat: 14g, Trans Fat: 0g) | Cholesterol: 70mg | Sodium: 60mg | Protein: 8g | Carbohydrate: 34g (Dietary Fiber: 3g) | Phosphorus: 120mg | Potassium: 200mg | Calcium: 150mg

Health Benefits

- Provides a good source of protein and antioxidants
- Can be a satisfying treat in moderation

Scientific Benefits

- Cocoa powder and dark chocolate are rich in flavonoids, which have been shown to support heart health and reduce inflammation.

Human Experience

"This Double Chocolate Chunk Gelato is a chocolate lover's dream. It's so creamy and rich, and the chocolate chunks add the perfect crunch."

Cautions and Precautions

- Be cautious when melting chocolate to avoid burning it and ruining the flavor.
- Check the expiration date of dairy products like milk and cream before using them in the recipe.
- Use high-quality chocolate to ensure rich and creamy texture in the gelato.
- Avoid over-mixing the chocolate chunks into the gelato mixture to maintain distinct chocolatey bites.

- Keep the gelato mixture refrigerated until ready to churn to prevent bacterial growth and foodborne illnesses.

Safety Measures

- Store the gelato in a shallow and wide container to minimize air exposure and prevent freezer burn.
- Keep the gelato container tightly sealed to prevent moisture loss and maintain its creamy texture.
- Store the gelato away from strong-smelling foods in the freezer to prevent flavor contamination.

White Chocolate Raspberry Gelato

A smooth and creamy gelato that combines the sweetness of white chocolate with the tartness of raspberries for a delightful contrast.

Ingredients:

- 2 cups whole milk
- 1 cup heavy cream
- 3/4 cup granulated sugar
- 1/2 cup white chocolate chips, melted
- 1 scoop vanilla protein powder
- 1 cup raspberries, fresh or frozen

Prep Time: 15 minutes **Freezing Time: 24 hours** **Serving Size: 4**

Instructions:

1. In a blender, combine the milk, cream, sugar, melted white chocolate chips, and protein powder. Blend until smooth.
2. Transfer the mixture into the Ninja Creami pint container.
3. Place the lid on the container and freeze for at least 24 hours.
4. After freezing, insert the container into the Ninja Creami machine.
5. Select the 'Gelato' program and start the machine.
6. Once the cycle is complete, check the consistency. If it's too thick, use the 'Re-spin' option.
7. Serve in bowls and enjoy the White Chocolate Raspberry Gelato!

Nutrition Information per Serving: Calories: 380 | Total Fat: 24g (Saturated Fat: 15g, Trans Fat: 0g) | Cholesterol: 80mg | Sodium: 80mg | Protein: 9g | Carbohydrate: 34g (Dietary Fiber: 2g) | Phosphorus: 140mg | Potassium: 220mg | Calcium: 160mg

Health Benefits

- Provides a good source of protein and antioxidants
- Raspberries are rich in vitamins and minerals, supporting overall health

Scientific Benefits

- White chocolate contains cocoa butter, which is rich in antioxidants and can have anti-inflammatory effects.
- Raspberries are high in ellagic acid, a compound that has been studied for its potential anti-cancer properties.

Human Experience

"The White Chocolate Raspberry Gelato is my favorite treat on a hot day. It's so refreshing and the combination of flavors is unbeatable."

Cautions and Precautions

- Be cautious when melting white chocolate to avoid overheating and seizing, which can ruin its texture.
- Check the freshness of raspberries and discard any moldy or mushy ones before adding them to the gelato mixture.
- Avoid over-blending the raspberries to maintain some texture and preserve their vibrant color in the gelato.

Safety Measures

- Transfer the gelato into individual serving containers to prevent the need for frequent opening of the main container.
- Place a layer of plastic wrap directly on the surface of the gelato before sealing the containers to prevent freezer burn.

- Store the gelato containers in the back of the freezer to maintain a consistent temperature and prevent thawing from frequent door openings.

Mint Chocolate Chip Gelato

A classic and refreshing gelato that perfectly balances the coolness of mint with the richness of chocolate chips.

Ingredients:

- 2 cups whole milk
- 1 cup heavy cream
- 3/4 cup granulated sugar
- 1 scoop vanilla protein powder
- 1 teaspoon peppermint extract
- 1/2 cup mini chocolate chips
- Green food coloring (optional)

Prep Time: 10 minutes **Freezing Time: 24 hours** **Serving Size: 4**

Instructions:

1. In a blender, combine the milk, cream, sugar, protein powder, and peppermint extract. Blend until smooth. You can include a few drops of green food coloring..
2. Transfer the mixture into the Ninja Creami pint container.
3. Place the lid on the container and freeze for at least 24 hours.
4. After freezing, insert the container into the Ninja Creami machine.
5. Select the 'Gelato' program and start the machine.
6. Once the cycle is complete, check the consistency. If it's too thick, use the 'Re-spin' option.
7. Serve in bowls and enjoy the Mint Chocolate Chip Gelato!

Nutrition Information per Serving: Calories: 360 | Total Fat: 22g (Saturated Fat: 14g, Trans Fat: 0g) | Cholesterol: 70mg | Sodium: 60mg | Protein: 8g | Carbohydrate: 34g (Dietary Fiber: 1g) | Phosphorus: 120mg | Potassium: 200mg | Calcium: 150mg

Health Benefits

- Offers a beneficial supply of protein and calcium.
- Serves as a delightful and revitalizing indulgence when consumed in moderation.

Scientific Benefits

- Peppermint extract has been shown to have digestive and antimicrobial properties.
- Chocolate contains flavonoids, which are antioxidants that can support heart health.

Human Experience

"The Mint Chocolate Chip Gelato is so creamy and flavorful. The mint is refreshing, and the chocolate chips add the perfect touch of sweetness."

Cautions and Precautions

- Be cautious when adding mint extract to the gelato mixture, as it can be overpowering if too much is used.
- Check the expiration date of dairy products like milk and cream before using them in the recipe.

Safety Measures

- Transfer the gelato into a shallow and wide container to facilitate easy scooping and serving.
- Store the gelato container on a stable surface in the freezer to prevent any spills or accidents.
- Avoid storing the gelato near the freezer door to prevent temperature fluctuations and maintain its consistency.

Chocolate Cherry Jubilee Gelato

A rich and indulgent gelato that combines the deep flavors of chocolate with the sweet tartness of cherries for a luxurious dessert.

Ingredients:

- 2 cups whole milk
- 1 cup heavy cream
- 3/4 cup granulated sugar
- 1/2 cup unsweetened cocoa powder

- 1 scoop chocolate protein powder
- 1 cup cherries, pitted and chopped
- 1/2 cup dark chocolate chunks

⏱ Prep Time: 15 minutes **⏱ Freezing Time: 24 hours** **🍽 Serving Size: 2**

Instructions:

1. In a blender, combine the milk, cream, sugar, cocoa powder, and protein powder. Blend until smooth.
2. Transfer the mixture into the Ninja Creami pint container. Add the chopped cherries and dark chocolate chunks, and mix gently to distribute evenly.
3. Place the lid on the container and freeze for at least 24 hours.
4. After freezing, insert the container into the Ninja Creami machine.
5. Select the 'Gelato' program and start the machine.
6. Once the cycle is complete, check the consistency. If it's too thick, use the 'Re-spin' option.
7. Serve in bowls and enjoy the Chocolate Cherry Jubilee Gelato!

Nutrition Information per Serving: Calories: 390 | Total Fat: 24g (Saturated Fat: 15g, Trans Fat: 0g) | Cholesterol: 80mg | Sodium: 70mg | Protein: 9g | Carbohydrate: 38g (Dietary Fiber: 4g) | Phosphorus: 140mg | Potassium: 250mg | Calcium: 160mg

Health Benefits

- Provides a good source of protein and antioxidants.
- Cherries are known for their anti-inflammatory properties and can aid in muscle recovery.

Scientific Benefits

- Cocoa powder and dark chocolate are rich in flavonoids, which have been shown to support heart health and reduce inflammation.
- Cherries contain anthocyanins, which are antioxidants that can help reduce inflammation and improve recovery from exercise.

Human Experience

" The Chocolate Cherry Jubilee Gelato offers a luxurious indulgence. It's perfect for when I'm craving something rich and satisfying. The blend of rich chocolate and succulent cherries creates an exquisite flavor experience!"

Cautions and Precautions

- Be cautious when melting chocolate to avoid burning it and ruining the flavor.
- Check the freshness of cherries and discard any bruised or moldy ones before using them in the recipe.

Safety Measures

- Transfer the gelato into smaller, individual containers to minimize air exposure and prevent freezer burn.
- Place the gelato containers in the coldest part of the freezer to ensure optimal freezing and preservation of texture.

Unique Flavor Combination

Espresso Hazelnut

A rich and creamy gelato that combines the bold flavor of espresso with the nutty taste of hazelnuts for a sophisticated treat.

Ingredients:

- 2 cups whole milk
- 1 cup heavy cream
- 3/4 cup granulated sugar
- 1 scoop vanilla protein powder
- 2 tablespoons espresso powder
- 1/2 cup hazelnuts, finely chopped

Prep Time: 15 minutes **Freezing Time: 24 hours** **Serving Size: 4**

Instructions:

1. In a blender, combine the milk, cream, sugar, protein powder, and espresso powder. Blend until smooth.

2. Transfer the mixture into the Ninja Creami pint container. Add the chopped hazelnuts and mix gently to distribute evenly.

3. Place the lid on the container and freeze for at least 24 hours.

4. After freezing, insert the container into the Ninja Creami machine.

5. Select the 'Gelato' program and start the machine.

6. Once the cycle is complete, check the consistency. If it's too thick, use the 'Re-spin' option.

7. Serve in bowls and enjoy the Espresso Hazelnut Gelato!

Nutrition Information per Serving: Calories: 380 | Total Fat: 22g (Saturated Fat: 12g, Trans Fat: 0g) | Cholesterol: 70mg | Sodium: 60mg | Protein: 10g | Carbohydrate: 36g (Dietary Fiber: 1g) | Phosphorus: 150mg | Potassium: 220mg | Calcium: 190mg

Health Benefits

- Provides a good source of protein and healthy fats
- Hazelnuts are rich in vitamins and minerals, supporting heart health

Scientific Benefits

- Espresso contains antioxidants and has been shown to improve mental alertness.
- Protein helps in muscle repair and growth, making this gelato a satisfying post-workout treat.

Human Experience

"The Espresso Hazelnut Gelato is my favorite way to indulge while still getting some protein. It's so rich and flavorful, and I love the crunch of the hazelnuts."

Cautions and Precautions

- Be cautious when brewing espresso to avoid over-extraction, which can result in a bitter flavor.
- Check the expiration date of dairy products like milk and cream before using them in the recipe.

Safety Measures

- Transfer the gelato into airtight containers to minimize air exposure and prevent ice crystals from forming.
- Store the gelato containers in a designated section of the freezer to prevent temperature fluctuations.

Almond Joy with Shredded Coconut Gelato

A delightful gelato that captures the essence of an Almond Joy candy bar, with a blend of almonds, coconut, and chocolate flavors.

Ingredients:

- 2 cups whole milk
- 1 cup heavy cream
- 3/4 cup granulated sugar
- 1 scoop chocolate protein powder
- 1/2 cup shredded coconut
- 1/2 cup almonds, chopped

Prep Time: 15 minutes   Freezing Time: 24 hours   Serving Size: 4

Instructions:

1. In a blender, combine the milk, cream, sugar, and protein powder. Blend until smooth.
2. Transfer the mixture into the Ninja Creami pint container. Add the shredded coconut and chopped almonds, and mix gently to distribute evenly.
3. Place the lid on the container and freeze for at least 24 hours.
4. After freezing, insert the container into the Ninja Creami machine.
5. Select the 'Gelato' program and start the machine.
6. Once the cycle is complete, check the consistency. If it's too thick, use the 'Re-spin' option.
7. Serve in bowls and enjoy the Almond Joy with Shredded Coconut Gelato!

Nutrition Information per Serving: Calories: 400 | Total Fat: 26g (Saturated Fat: 16g, Trans Fat: 0g) | Cholesterol: 80mg | Sodium: 70mg | Protein: 10g | Carbohydrate: 36g (Dietary Fiber: 2g) | Phosphorus: 170mg | Potassium: 240mg | Calcium: 200mg

Health Benefits

- Provides a good source of protein and healthy fats
- Almonds and coconut are known for their heart-healthy benefits

Scientific Benefits

- Chocolate protein powder provides essential amino acids for muscle repair.
- Almonds contain vitamin E and healthy fats that can help lower cholesterol levels.

Human Experience

"This gelato is like a tropical vacation in a bowl. The combination of coconut and almonds is so satisfying, and the chocolate protein powder adds a nice touch of sweetness."

Cautions and Precautions

- Be cautious when toasting coconut to avoid burning it and ruining the flavor.
- Avoid over-chopping the almonds to maintain their crunchiness and prevent them from turning mushy in the gelato.
- Store the gelato away from foods with strong odors to preserve its almond joy flavor.

Safety Measures

- Transfer the gelato into shallow containers to facilitate easy scooping and serving.
- Store the gelato containers in a freezer with consistent temperature to maintain its texture and flavor.

Peanut Butter and Banana Blast with Chia Seeds Gelato

A creamy and nutritious gelato that combines the classic flavors of peanut butter and banana, enhanced with the added crunch of chia seeds.

Ingredients:

- 2 cups whole milk

- 1 cup heavy cream
- 3/4 cup granulated sugar
- 1 scoop vanilla protein powder
- 1/2 cup natural peanut butter
- 1 ripe banana, mashed
- 2 tablespoons chia seeds

⏲**Prep Time: 10 minutes** ⏲ **Freezing Time: 24 hours** 🍽 **Serving Size: 4**

Instructions:

1. In a blender, combine the milk, cream, sugar, protein powder, peanut butter, and mashed banana. Blend until smooth.
2. Transfer the mixture into the Ninja Creami pint container. Add the chia seeds and mix gently to distribute evenly.
3. Place the lid on the container and freeze for at least 24 hours.
4. After freezing, insert the container into the Ninja Creami machine.
5. Select the 'Gelato' program and start the machine.
6. Once the cycle is complete, check the consistency. If it's too thick, use the 'Re-spin' option.
7. Serve in bowls and enjoy the Peanut Butter and Banana Blast with Chia Seeds Gelato!

Nutrition Information per Serving: Calories: 420 | Total Fat: 26g (Saturated Fat: 14g, Trans Fat: 0g) | Cholesterol: 85mg | Sodium: 150mg | Protein: 12g | Carbohydrate: 38g (Dietary Fiber: 4g) | Phosphorus: 200mg | Potassium: 320mg | Calcium: 220mg

Health Benefits

- Provides a good source of protein and healthy fats
- Chia seeds boast plentiful omega-3 fatty acids and fiber.

Scientific Benefits

- Peanut butter contains monounsaturated fats, which are beneficial for heart health.
- Chia seeds have been shown to improve digestive health and reduce inflammation.

Human Experience

"The Peanut Butter and Banana Blast gelato is a game-changer. It's so creamy and satisfying, and I love the added crunch from the chia seeds. It's my go-to treat when I want something sweet and healthy."

Cautions and Precautions

- Use caution when adding chia seeds to the mixture, ensuring they are evenly distributed to avoid clumping.
- Keep the gelato mixture chilled while preparing to prevent the bananas from browning.
- Store the gelato away from foods with strong odors to preserve its peanut butter and banana flavor.

Safety Measures

- Transfer the gelato into shallow, freezer-safe containers to facilitate even freezing and easy scooping.
- Store the gelato containers in the back of the freezer to maintain a consistent temperature and prevent thawing.
- Avoid overcrowding the freezer with other items to allow proper air circulation around the gelato containers.

	BRAKFAST	LUNCH	DINNER
DAY 1	Tropical Paradise Milkshake	Berry Protein Power Bowl	Strawberry Cheesecake Delight
DAY 2	Mango Protein Sorbet	Tropical Muscle Builder	Blackberry Lavender Bliss
DAY 3	Green Dream Milkshake	Green Warrior Bowl	Blueberry Muffin Magic
DAY 4	Blueberry Protein Sorbet	Antioxidant Acai Boost	Chocolate Chip Cookie Dough Dream
DAY 5	Pumpkin Spice Protein Delight Milkshake	Pumpkin Spice Recovery Bowl	S'mores Sensation
DAY 6	Double Chocolate Chunk Gelato	Mango Lassi Lift	Pistachio Paradise
DAY 7	Strawberry Banana Protein Sorbet	Blueberry Maple Muscle	Salted Caramel Pretzel
DAY 8	Coconut Lime Protein Sorbet	Sunrise Citrus Surge	Coffee Almond Crunch
DAY 9	Almond Chocolate Protein Sorbet	Peanut Butter Cup Pro Bowl	Snickerdoodle Surprise
DAY 10	White Chocolate Raspberry Gelato	Cafe Mocha Energizer	Birthday Cake Bash
DAY 11	Matcha Green Tea Protein Sorbet	Tropical Paradise Gelato	Peanut Butter and Banana Blast with Chia Seeds Gelato
DAY 12	Berry Blast Milkshake	Peanut Butter Powerhouse Milkshake	Chocolate Cherry Jubilee Gelato

DAY 13	Lavender Honey Protein Sorbet	Coconut Lime Protein Sorbet	Cookies & Cream Craze Milkshake
DAY 14	Espresso Hazelnut Gelato	Berry Protein Power Bowl	Peanut Butter Powerhouse Milkshake
DAY 15	Watermelon Mint Marvel	Green Warrior Bowl	Pistachio Paradise
DAY 16	Blueberry Protein Sorbet	Chocolate Chip Cookie Dough Dream	Salted Caramel Pretzel
DAY 17	Cafe Mocha Energizer	Tropical Muscle Builder	Birthday Cake Bash
DAY 18	Mango Protein Sorbet	Peanut Butter Cup Pro Bowl	Snickerdoodle Surprise
DAY 19	Matcha Mint Marvel Milkshake	Antioxidant Acai Boost	S'mores Sensation
DAY 20	Peanut Butter and Banana Blast with Chia Seeds Gelato	Berry Blast Milkshake	Chocolate Cherry Jubilee Milkshake
DAY 21	Tropical Paradise Gelato	Green Dream Milkshake	Strawberry Cheesecake Delight

APPENDIX 1: RECIPE INDEX

VOLUME EQUIVALENT (DRY)

US Standard Measurement	Metric Equivalents
1/4 teaspoon	1.23 ml
1/2 teaspoon	2.46 ml
3/4 teaspoon	3.69 ml
1 teaspoon	4.93 ml
2 teaspoons	9.86 ml
1 tablespoon	14.79 ml
1/4 cup	59.15 ml
1/2 cup	118.3 ml
3/4 cup	177.45 ml
1 cup	236.6 ml
2 cups	473.2 ml
3 cups	709.8 ml
4 cups	946.4 ml

VOLUME EQUIVALENT (LIQUID)

US Standard (Imperial)	Metric (SI)
1 fluid ounce (fl oz)	29.574 milliliters (ml)
1 cup	236.588 milliliters (ml)
1 pint (16 fl oz)	473.176 milliliters (ml)
1 quart (32 fl oz)	946.353 milliliters (ml)
1 gallon (128 fl oz)	3.785 liters (L)
1 tablespoon	14.787 milliliters (ml)
1 teaspoon	4.929 milliliters (ml)
1 milliliter (ml)	0.0338 fluid ounces (fl oz)
1 liter (L)	33.814 fluid ounces (fl oz)
1 liter (L)	1.0567 quarts
1 liter (L)	0.26417 gallons

TEMPERATURE EQUIVALENT

Fahrenheit (°F)	Celsius (°C)
225 °F	107 °C
250 °F	120 °C
275 °F	135 °C
300 °F	150 °C
325 °F	160 °C
350 °F	180 °C
375 °F	190 °C
400 °F	205 °C
425 °F	220 °C
450 °F	235 °C
475 °F	245 °C
500 °F	260 °C

WEIGHT MEASUREMENT

Ingredient	US Standard	Metric
1/2 ounce	14.175 grams	
1 ounce	28.35 grams	30 mL
2 ounces	60 grams	60 mL
5 ounces	150 grams	150 mL
10 ounces	300 grams	300 mL
16 ounces	450 grams	450 mL
1 pound	454 grams	454 mL
1.5 pounds	681 grams	681 mL
2 pounds	907 grams	907 mL

APPENDIX 3: RECIPE JOURNAL

Date: _____

Recipe Title:

Ingredients: **Notes**   **Description**

\- - - - - - - - - - - - - - - - - - -   \- - - - - - - - - - - - - - - - - - -

\- - - - - - - - - - - - - - - - - - -   \- - - - - - - - - - - - - - - - - - -

\- - - - - - - - - - - - - - - - - - -   \- - - - - - - - - - - - - - - - - - -

\- - - - - - - - - - - - - - - - - - -   \- - - - - - - - - - - - - - - - - - -

\- - - - - - - - - - - - - - - - - - -   \- - - - - - - - - - - - - - - - - - -

\- - - - - - - - - - - - - - - - - - -   \- - - - - - - - - - - - - - - - - - -

\- - - - - - - - - - - - - - - - - - -   \- - - - - - - - - - - - - - - - - - -

\- - - - - - - - - - - - - - - - - - -   \- - - - - - - - - - - - - - - - - - -

\- - - - - - - - - - - - - - - - - - -   \- - - - - - - - - - - - - - - - - - -

\- - - - - - - - - - - - - - - - - - -   \- - - - - - - - - - - - - - - - - - -

\- - - - - - - - - - - - - - - - - - -   \- - - - - - - - - - - - - - - - - - -

\- - - - - - - - - - - - - - - - - - -   \- - - - - - - - - - - - - - - - - - -

\- - - - - - - - - - - - - - - - - - -   \- - - - - - - - - - - - - - - - - - -

\- - - - - - - - - - - - - - - - - - -

Prep time: **Total time:**   \- - - - - - - - - - - - - - - - - - -

\- - - - - - - - - - - - - - - - - - -

\- - - - - - - - - - - - - - - - - - -

Date: _____

Recipe Title:

Ingredients: Notes   Description

------------------------   ------------------------------
------------------------   ------------------------------
------------------------   ------------------------------
------------------------   ------------------------------
------------------------   ------------------------------
------------------------   ------------------------------
------------------------   ------------------------------
------------------------   ------------------------------
------------------------   ------------------------------
------------------------   ------------------------------
------------------------   ------------------------------
------------------------   ------------------------------
------------------------   ------------------------------

Prep time: Total time:

Date: _____

Recipe Title:

Ingredients:	Notes	Description
----------------------		----------------------------
----------------------		----------------------------
----------------------		----------------------------
----------------------		----------------------------
----------------------		----------------------------
----------------------		----------------------------
----------------------		----------------------------
----------------------		----------------------------
----------------------		----------------------------
----------------------		----------------------------
----------------------		----------------------------
----------------------		----------------------------
----------------------		----------------------------
----------------------		----------------------------

Prep time: **Total time:**

Date: _____

Recipe Title:

Ingredients: *Notes*   *Description*

---------------------------   ---------------------------
---------------------------   ---------------------------
---------------------------   ---------------------------
---------------------------   ---------------------------
---------------------------   ---------------------------
---------------------------   ---------------------------
---------------------------   ---------------------------
---------------------------   ---------------------------
---------------------------   ---------------------------
---------------------------   ---------------------------
---------------------------   ---------------------------
---------------------------   ---------------------------
---------------------------   ---------------------------

Prep time: *Total time:*

Date: _____

Recipe Title:

Ingredients: Notes   Description

-------------------------   -------------------------
-------------------------   -------------------------
-------------------------   -------------------------
-------------------------   -------------------------
-------------------------   -------------------------
-------------------------   -------------------------
-------------------------   -------------------------
-------------------------   -------------------------
-------------------------   -------------------------
-------------------------   -------------------------
-------------------------   -------------------------
-------------------------   -------------------------
-------------------------   -------------------------

Prep time: Total time:

Made in United States
Orlando, FL
03 December 2024

54943039R00061